Pagan Portals
Nature Mystics

The Literary Gateway to Modern Paganism

Pagan Portals
Nature Mystics

The Literary Gateway to Modern Paganism

Rebecca Beattie

MOON
BOOKS

Winchester, UK
Washington, USA

First published by Moon Books, 2015
Moon Books is an imprint of John Hunt Publishing Ltd., Laurel House, Station Approach,
Alresford, Hants, SO24 9JH, UK
office1@jhpbooks.net
www.johnhuntpublishing.com
www.moon-books.net

For distributor details and how to order please visit the 'Ordering' section on our website.

ISBN: 978 1 78279 799 9
Library of Congress Control Number: 2015930998

A CIP catalogue record for this book is available from the British Library.

Design: Lee Nash

Printed and bound by CPI Group (UK) Ltd, Croydon, CR0 4YY, UK

We operate a distinctive and ethical publishing philosophy in all
areas of our business, from our global network of authors to
production and worldwide distribution.

CONTENTS

For all those Nature Mystics who have come before and continue to inspire us to a spiritual path with their words.

Acknowledgements

This is really my space for thanking the people without whom this book would not have been possible and those who contributed thoughts and ideas along the way. Firstly to Trevor Greenfield at Moon Books for supporting a slightly kookie idea and giving me the space and confidence to develop it in the way that I wanted to. Without Trevor's support, this book would probably have not made it through the selection process. Secondly, I would like to thank my familial army of Nature Mystic readers and proofreaders who helped me to read and ensure I was writing what I had intended to write. That army was a small but very efficient one – David Beattie, Mary Beattie and Kath Beattie. I also need to thank Lizzie Conrad-Hughes, Nature Mystic extraordinaire, for the many discussions we had in Lincoln's Inn Fields about who should be included and who should not. Lizzie contributed many of the ideas for the writers in the series and also edited with zeal and panache. Also thanks to Ewis who doesn't just encourage me in my writing, but takes for granted that I will write lots of books, and inspires me to think the same way too. I must also thank Christina Oakley-Harrington, dear friend and founder of Treadwell's Bookshop and Cultural Centre in Bloomsbury, London. Without Christina, I would never have found my words or the confidence to speak them aloud.

I would also like to thank those of you who read the Moon Books Blog on Nature Mystics that led to this becoming a book. You also contributed ideas and thoughts along the way, on who you wanted to read about, and who should not have been forgotten. Keats made it to the final list because of your input, and it was lovely to write a book by way of a two-way conversation.

If you have enjoyed this book and would like to find out more, or for more information about my writing and research, you can find me at

www.rebeccabeattie.co.uk,

on Facebook at

https://www.facebook.com/Rebeccabeattie13

or on Twitter at

https://twitter.com/rebecca_beattie

There is also a collection of photos of our Nature Mystics at

http://uk.pinterest.com/rebeccambeattie/nature-mystics/

Feedback is always a wonderful thing, positive or otherwise. Please do get in touch, as I would love to hear from you. Also, reviews on websites such as Amazon are always really important to a writer, as they can really help other people make the decision to read your work, and will encourage the writer to keep writing! If you have loved this book and would like to help others find it, please do leave reviews on Amazon or on Goodreads or anywhere else you feel able to.

Introduction

When I was fifteen, I fell in love with Kester Woodseaves, who was a weaver. He was everything a young girl just emerging into womanhood could want. He was kind, saw beyond physical imperfections, and recognised the soul beneath. He was infinitely wise: to Kester, caterpillars were 'butterflies as is to be', he abhorred cruelty in any shape (particularly towards animals) and he recognised the divine influence in nature. There was only one drawback: Kester was in love with Prue Sarn, and they were both perfectly suited to each other. And they were both fictional characters.

Mary Webb's novel *Precious Bane* tells the story of Prue Sarn: doomed to a facial disfigurement when her mother is cursed by a hare, Prue is taught to read by the local cunning man, since she was believed to be too ugly to marry. But Prue lives in superstitious times, and whispers of 'witch' follow her wherever she goes. Local logic dictates that the outside appearance must be a reflection of what lies within. With her gentle ways and her piercing observations of both nature and human nature, Prue is a character who intrigued me. As a young woman on the path to Modern Paganism, she became someone I could relate to, someone I could look to for inspiration. She saw the world in the same way I did.

While I might never meet them in the flesh, Prue and Kester's story was one I would return to again and again over the years, as it is haunting and very beautiful. Not satisfied with *Precious Bane* alone, I then turned to every other Mary Webb novel I could find, and discovered that she had written novels, poems and essays, all following the common theme of the healing and inspirational properties of nature, all served up with a large portion of folklore.

Time has inevitably flowed on, and some twenty five years

later, I am in the fortunate position of carrying out post graduate research on Mary Webb. One of the most common things said of her is that she was a 'Nature Mystic', which helps me to make sense of why I was so drawn to her all those years ago. A 'Nature Mystic', simply put, is someone who has mystical experiences in nature, or connects to the divine through nature, and uses that connection as fuel for inspiration. The sense of what that divine looks like may change from Nature Mystic to Nature Mystic, but their sense of the sacred value of the natural world is less likely to. This undoubtedly has much in common with the myriad pagan paths (although Nature Mystics can come from any religious background and are not bound by any one particular belief system). The difficulty I had in the early days of my research, was in knowing how to place Mary Webb amongst her peers. She does not meet the usual standards required for tradi-tional classification in literature. While her contemporaries were immersed in urban Modernism, Webb was steadfastly rural; while traditionally rural writers looked back to the past for their belief systems, Webb wrote about distinctly modern themes like sex without marriage, and the role of women in society. And all with an undeniable, unmistakable undercurrent of the occult that cannot be ignored. Webb is a distinctly lunar-shaped peg in a world of square holes.

In my search to place Mary Webb, I became curious, and my research also led me to look at other writers. Who else wrote like Webb? Which other writers were also Nature Mystics? (Or at least, if not strictly Nature Mystics, then deeply inspired by nature.) Who else wrote about nature in the very moving way that Webb did? Rather unsurprisingly, there are many authors with a deep tie to the natural world. Webb wrote in the early twentieth century, and bucked the trend of her Modernist contemporaries (like Virginia Woolf and F. Scott Fitzgerald) by sticking to her rural roots in Shropshire, although she lived in London for a time. Her predecessors and influences could be seen to be the Romantic writers, such as Wordsworth, Coleridge and Keats, or Thomas Hardy, so that was where my trail started. But along the way I discovered a few surprises, and a few writers (like Webb) who had largely been forgotten over the years. I realised that the writers I was exploring were significant for several reasons. Not only did all of the writers (except Keats) bridge the gap between the Victorian period and Modernism (two very different zeitgeists), but they also showed signs of being proto-pagan. The writers were too early to be considered Modern Pagans since they were writing before the rise of Modern Paganism that was heralded by the repeal of the Witchcraft Act in 1951, or the publication of Gerald Gardner's *Witchcraft Today* in 1954. However, all of them found periods of great popularity in the 1930s and 1940s, and they all contributed to the pre-pagan cultural environment that allowed people like Gardner to explore paganism as a world view. While it might be too big a leap to suggest that Webb or her peers were early members of that movement, each of them was influential in the key decades in which an English popular sensibility for pagan spirituality was brewing. For instance, Webb's work only found its way to the bestsellers lists after her death in 1927, and her novels were hugely popular throughout the 1930s, 1940s and 1950s, at a time when the countryside revival was in full swing, and the beginnings of Modern Paganism were starting to stir in the imagination of its founders. John Keats is our one anomaly in this study, in that he is a precursor to all of the writers, and of a very different time. But all of the later writers, without exception, were influenced in some way by the Romantics. If this were an academic study I would have left Keats out as he is 'out of time', but the readers of the Nature Mystics blog that led to this book, were adamant that they wanted him left in.

Scholars are now starting to take an interest in Webb and some of her lesser known peers such as Mary Butts and Sylvia Townsend Warner. Like them, Modern Paganism, too, is in its academic youth. While we could question the relevance of academia to our own spiritual practices, I believe that both subject areas deserve more attention than they have been given in the past, and we still look to academia to confirm credibility. Scholars are examining the twentieth century pagan revival, and are uncovering and rediscovering the writings and art that created the environment in which a Modern Pagan movement could come into existence. While this movement has not yet received much academic interest within a literary context, both Ronald Hutton and Susan Greenwood have led the examination of the development of Modern Paganism (Hutton from a historical point of view, and Greenwood from that of anthropology). Hutton led this effort with his pioneering 1999 work *The Triumph of the Moon*. Since then the details have been filling out further. Significantly, Hutton notes that Modern Paganism is a movement that was born from literature. For instance, he writes that Modern Paganism's 'seasonal rites were largely a pastiche of existing literary texts' that were designed to counteract the influence of modernity, by 'connecting human beings to the rhythm of the seasons, and thus – traditionally – to the supernatural forces that may lie behind it'[1]. Hutton also identifies certain other key concepts that contributed to the emergence of Modern Paganism, concepts such as reverence for the countryside and the desire to conserve it, a fascination with folklore, interest in historical figures such as cunning folk, and the Hellenic past (influenced by the work of anthropologist Jane Harrison). So in order to be considered properly proto-pagan, our Nature Mystics *should* counteract Modernity by connecting us to both the turning seasons, and the wheel of the year, as well as connecting us to the divine that lies behind it.

For me, this linked Webb's writing directly to my own Wiccan path. The connection I had felt when first reading Webb was there academically as well. All of these elements were evident in *Precious Bane*. I had found my answer, and it was much closer to home than I would have anticipated.

For the purpose of this book, I have identified ten writers to explore, although there are countless others. I realise this is a very narrow field of focus, but what interests me is the idea that the literature of the late Victorian age and early twentieth century became part of that 'pastiche of existing literary texts' that found their way into pagan rituals. Keats has found his place among the Nature Mystics, despite being out of time with the rest of them, as he has been such an influence on the writers who came after him. For me he presents the proto-proto-pagan if you like. If this was an academic book, I would be criticised for including him, but publishing this outside of academia gives me a little more freedom to play with my definitions. Although I acknowledge that I flit in and out of academia in my work, this is clearly not an academic book. In this project I wear the hat of a practitioner, who is exploring our literary past and origins. And speaking of definitions, I deliberately use the term 'Modern Paganism' as a loose one, and as a way of including all of the myriad different paths that sit under that umbrella. To identify all of the sources and nuances of each pagan path would take more space than is available in this series. So if you follow a Wiccan Path, or a Heathen one, or that of a Druid, all routes commonly connect to nature, just as the Nature Mystics in this book do. And if you do not identify as one who follows a pagan path, but do connect to the divine in nature, I do not wish to exclude you either. Perhaps this study might pique your curiosity or show similarities between all of us.

As this book is in the Pagan Portals series, it is intended to be an introduction, and not a full and comprehensive literary research project. I hope it will stimulate your own curiosity to explore some of these writers further, and maybe approach your own reading from a slightly different perspective to the one we may have been taught in the education system where you lived. The clues to a hidden heritage are out there in the books we studied at school, but also in the books we weren't taught, and from the writers who disappeared from the literary canon. Some of them are beginning to make their way back into the consciousness of academia, and they are worthy of more focus.

I have selected as many women writers as male, deliberately because of my own interest in woman writers, and for balance. And some of them are more pagan than others. They are: John Keats, Mary Webb, Thomas Hardy, Sylvia Townsend Warner, D.H. Lawrence, Elizabeth von Arnim, William Butler Yeats, Mary Butts, J.R.R. Tolkien and Edith Nesbit. Some may be more familiar than others, but it is hoped that this journey will enable you to see some of the more well-known writers through a fresh lens. English literature classes in school may have left an impression that Thomas Hardy always wrote tragic endings, or that D.H. Lawrence had questionable views about women; but they also wrote some of the most stirring descriptions of nature, and connected to nature in ways that will be recognisable to those who seek a deep connection with the natural world. D.H. Lawrence, for instance, always liked to write while sitting beneath a tree; Elizabeth von Arnim connected to nature through her garden; E. Nesbit wrote while sitting in a boat at her moated home; while Mary Webb meditated on details in nature for hours on end while composing her novels and poems. And all of them led quite extraordinary lives.

Some of the writers were more overtly esoteric than others. For instance, W.B. Yeats and E. Nesbit were both active members of the Hermetic Order of the Golden Dawn, while Mary Butts had a relationship with Aleister Crowley (albeit one that ended rather acrimoniously). Others, like Tolkien, followed a path very different to paganism, but also demonstrate some very pagan themes, and undoubtedly influenced Modern Paganism's winding myriad paths.

It is possible that to some degree all of the writers in this series could be seen to have pantheistic leanings, or mystical tendencies, but labels are often difficult to affix, and sometimes even harder to shake off, so I use the terms loosely. In these chapters, I will explore a little of their lives, their beliefs, their connections to nature, and of course their writing, and how it might be relevant to someone on a pagan path in the twenty-first century.

John Keats (1795 – 1821)

John Keats is often cited as a seminal influence on many of the other writers in this series. Therefore, before turning to the other writers in this series who occupied the late nineteenth and early twentieth centuries, it is worth jumping back in time to the late Regency period in order to examine Keats' work and find out why Keats was so influential, and how his work relates to the spectrum of pantheists and other nature worshipping traditions. Reaching beyond the musings of my fifteen-year-old self who had heavily annotated my copy of *Selected Letters and Poems of Keats*, this particular exploration has yielded some surprises.

Keats represents the second generation of Romantic poets, coming hard on the heels of the first generation, Wordsworth and Coleridge, who published their trailblazing *Lyrical Ballads* in 1797. The Romantics are often referred to as pantheists, the belief system that states that god or the divine (the 'theism' part) is found everywhere (the 'pan' part), but such definitions are never clear cut. Wordsworth leaned more towards a Christian pantheism, while Coleridge experimented more with mysticism (and opium) most famously writing 'Kubla Khan' on awakening from an opium trip. This is where John Keats puts rather a spanner in the works of anyone hoping for a neat classification. His own belief system is misty, ineffable, and not clearly defined beyond his love of poetry and beauty, and his love of love. Keats did not just look to nature for inspiration, but rather to human nature; his muse was more often found in human behaviour (often his own) and also in the emotional storms of his life (of which there were many). Keats lived and loved with a passion, but also battled the black dog of depression throughout his life. If one were to identify an overarching theme in his work, it would probably be his quest for self-knowledge. For anyone on a spiritual path for any length of time, this theme cannot fail to resonate. John Keats is less of a Nature Mystic, and more a 'Human Nature Mystic'; a writer who endeavoured to 'know thyself', as the sign at the entrance to the Delphic Oracle once instructed. His path as a Nature Mystic was an inward looking one, instead of one that looked outwards to the natural world for inspiration.

Keats' Life: Putting his Work in Context

It is often apparent that the lives of great writers were more dramatic than fiction, and John Keats is no exception. Born in 1795 in London, his family life was somewhat tempestuous. His father was killed in a riding accident when John was only nine years old, leaving his mother in financial difficulty. She remarried within two months, and when her own father died, she entered into a very acrimonious lawsuit against her mother over her father's estate. Within two years of her second marriage, she and her husband separated, and she sent her children to live with the grandmother she had fallen out with. John Keats was the eldest of four children, and he and his two brothers were sent to school in Enfield. When he was thirteen, his mother and grandmother were reconciled, and his mother came to live with them. The reunion was short-lived, as she contracted tuberculosis and died a year later. The young John (then fourteen) had been in charge of her nursing, and took her loss very badly. Later that year, he left school and was apprenticed to a surgeon, but the relationship was stormy, and Keats later left his residence, to train instead at Guy's Hospital. By all accounts he became very skilled in medicine.

It was in his late teenage years that Keats discovered poetry, by spending much of his spare time with an old school friend who had remained in formal education. Keats was introduced to the work of Spenser, which inspired him to write his first poem, aged eighteen. The next few years were spent absorbed in poetry, as he experimented with different forms. In 1816 (at the age of twenty one) he obtained a license to practice as an apothecary, but he became more and more convinced that his calling was to be a poet, not a doctor. By the time he received his license, his grandmother had died, and his financial affairs had been left in the care of a trustee. The trustee had embezzled Keats' money, convinced that he wouldn't need the money if he was to be practicing the affluent profession of medicine. This had long-lasting effects on Keats, who struggled financially for the rest of his life. Unknown to anyone at the time, his maternal grandfather had left a trust fund, which would have solved this problem, but no one knew of its existence until later.

In 1816 (when Keats was twenty one) he met Leigh Hunt, which was to be a life-changing event. Hunt had published some of Keats' work in *The Examiner*, and meeting Hunt opened up a new world of experience for him. He was now moving in literary circles, and his social group included writers such as Byron and Shelley. This gave Keats the momentum he needed to give up medicine forever, in favour of being a poet. Wordsworth and Coleridge had stormed onto the literary scene, publishing the *Lyrical Ballads* in 1797, as a reaction against the lofty language and highly structured work of the Augustan school, as typified by writers like Pope. By contrast, the Romantics set out to use common language, and freer forms of poetry, like the 'ballads' of Wordsworth and Coleridge's title. The first generation of Romantics also explored ideas of pantheism, although Wordsworth later returned to a form of Christian pantheism; Coleridge was more inclined to mysticism, and (for the sake of the title of this series) was probably more of a Nature Mystic than any of his peers. Keats was greatly influenced by both Wordsworth and Coleridge (although they had a somewhat strained personal relationship). The second generation continued to work in opposition to the approach of the classical school, and placed more emphasis on the value of emotional responses over rational enlightenment.

Keats' career as a poet was very short lived, as it really only lasted five years. To begin with, his poetry received mixed reviews, but his faith in his ability enabled him to continue, somewhat presciently stating that he thought he would become a great poet after his death. In 1818, Keats set off on a walking tour of Scotland with a friend, but returned home to Hampstead early as he was unwell. On returning, he found his brother very obviously dying with tuberculosis, and stayed to nurse him, whilst composing his epic poem, 'Hyperion'. When his brother died, Keats moved to Wentworth Place, to live with Charles Brown. This house has since been re-named Keats House, and now houses the Keats museum.

But the drama of Keats' life was by no means over. Soon after he moved to Wentworth Place, the Brawne family moved into the other half of the house. Keats fell in love with Fanny Brawne, and wrote some of his most impassioned work for her, such as 'Bright Star', and 'The Eve of Saint Agnes'. Following his brother's death, Keats entered a period of depression and restlessness, in which he wrote long and tortured letters to Fanny Brawne, desperate to be with her, but unable to marry because of his financial difficulties. A short while later, Keats became ill again, and this time he soon suspected he was suffering from latent tuberculosis, contracted whilst nursing his brother, although doctors told him he had nothing to fear. He knew the symptoms very well and also knew the prognosis was not good, having now nursed two family members through the disease. His final year was one of great pain and anguish, since doctors would not agree on a diagnosis, and therefore did little to alleviate his discomfort and suffering. In late 1820 it was decided he would benefit from spending the winter in Italy, so he and a friend set out for Rome, but it was there that he died in February 1821, at the age of just twenty six.

Keats was buried in Rome, with his chosen epitaph carved on his headstone, so clearly indicative of one who has walked a spiritual path of seeking self-knowledge. It read, 'Here lies one whose name was writ in water'.

Keats and Spirituality

While a Nature Mystic is essentially someone who connects to the divine through the natural world, there is little evidence to suggest that Keats did this, although his descriptions of nature are highly evocative (as are all of his descriptions of beauty in the world). Nature is an obvious source of beauty, and as such is written about in Keats' poetry, but whether he saw this as a way of connecting to the divine is not immediately obvious. Unlike Mary Webb, Keats did not appear to meditate in nature in order to find inspiration; he was a city dweller all his life, although the outlying parts of London he lived in (such as Hampstead and Enfield) would have been far less urban than they might be considered today. He did, however, find endless fascination in human behaviour, and was very much on a spiritual quest to know himself, and his own behaviour. Robert Gittings (one of Keats' biographers) suggests that Keats used his correspondence with close friends and family as a form of spiritual journal, recording over time a clear pattern of development. In his letters, Keats often ruminates over the processes in which he has reached various philosophical conclusions, and examines his own thought processes in great detail. Gittings also concludes that Keats' self-awareness was second to none for a young man of such intense feeling. Not surprisingly, he also had an innate sense of the tragedy of life.

Keats' upbringing with his grandmother was a Christian one, but later in life, his Christian faith dwindled and changed, according to Andrew Motion (the former poet laureate, and one of Keats' more recent biographers). His personal faith system is quite hazy, and is difficult to define clearly. Keats did dissent from organised religion, and instead is said to have favoured a more 'natural' religion. This would broadly be defined as the belief that divinity is part of nature, and not separate from it. But his only incontrovertible declarations of faith were in poetry, beauty, and love (both physical and spiritual), and his most consistent belief was in his calling as a poet.

Critics often have a polarised view of Keats' philosophy. Some biographers believe he was essentially a man of science (as a result of his medical training) and clearly a humanist, while others ascribe a profoundly mystical path. One study by Jennifer Wunder has examined his links to Hermeticism and secret societies, such as the Rosicrucian order and Freemasonry, and has found a consistent pattern of hermetic imagery within his poetry. Wunder points out that Keats' quest to know himself was also reflective of the initiatory system of secret societies, where one increased one's own self-knowledge while progressing through the degrees. She identifies his intended path as being one where he 'was to move from human passions to knowledge and transmute that knowledge to poetry that might provide physical to men'[2]. Keats declared that he wanted to use his poetry to heal people, and by doing so, be 'one who pours out a balm upon the world'.

While there is no clear evidence to suggest that Keats was actually a member of the Rosicrucian Fraternity or the Freemasons, the imagery used by both movements shows up repeatedly in his poetry and his letters, so much so that it is too clear to be passed off as a coincidence. For example, his epic poem 'Hyperion' is sometimes interpreted as an initiation which shares much in common with those of the secret societies; from preparation through to the actual rite (which takes the form of a symbolic death and re-birth) followed by a period of re-integration, and continued learning through different stages. The same study also points out there may be several explanations for the hermetic imagery, aside from Keats having actually been a member of either movement. During his medical training at Guy's Hospital, Keats became firm friends with a fellow student,

John Spurgin, who was a follower of the Swedish philosopher and Christian mystic, Emanuel Swedenborg, and discussed these philosophies at great length with Keats, as well as the hermetic philosophies. Wunder also suggests that the popularity of secret societies such as the Freemasons at this time meant that the philosophical ideas behind the movements, and the blending of Hermeticism and Neo-Platonism were commonly known within society. This in turn filtered into the arts, and was explored in gothic novels and other romantic literature, particularly in the work of those who influenced Keats, such as Coleridge, Burns and Hunt. While the Rosicrucians and the Freemasons may have been secret societies, they looked to similar alchemical and philosophical texts for inspiration. These books, such as works by Cornelius Agrippa, Hermes Trismegistus, Marsilio Ficino and Paracelsus, were also commonly read by Keats' contemporaries, particularly while studying (as Keats did) to become a doctor or an apothecary. Keats may not have allied himself with one particular definable religion or philosophy, but it does not mean he wasn't interested in them. Wunder concludes that during the Romantic period, mysticism and secularisation existed side by side in Masonic organisations, so it is possible to conclude that this may have disseminated out into wider society.

While Keats is considered to be fluent in the language of hermetic traditions, his only declared religious feelings were towards poetry, beauty and love. One of Keats' most often quoted philosophies comes from 'Ode on a Grecian Urn' where Keats writes:

Beauty is truth, truth beauty, – that is all
Ye know on earth, and all Ye need to know.

Additionally, in a letter to Fanny Brawne in October 1819, towards the end of his short life, Keats wrote:

I have been astonished that men could die martyrs for religion – I have shudder'd at it – I shudder no more – I could be martyr'd for my Religion – love is my religion – I could die for that – I could die for you. My creed is love and you are its only tenet.

Keats' Written Work

Keats work is remarkably extensive, for such a relatively short career. His oeuvre consists of both his poems and his recorded letters, and while it might be tempting to read only his poetry, his letters make for an enlightening context for the poems, and there is merit in reading them alongside each other. Keats experimented in several poetic forms during his career. Keats much admired Shakespeare, and consequently spent some time emulating the sonnets. Later he experimented with longer epic poems, such as in 'Hyperion' and 'Lamia'. His best known work comes from his later period, when he began to work with 'Odes'. 'Ode to a Nightingale' is one of his best known:

> Darkling I listen; and for many a time
> I have been half in love with easeful Death
> Call'd him soft names in many a mused rhyme,
> To take into the air my quiet breath

'Ode on a Grecian Urn' is equally remembered:

> Thou still unravish'd bride of quietness,
> Thou foster-child of silence and slow time,

But possibly the most well-known work by Keats (which often people know without realising) is 'To Autumn':

> Season of mists and mellow fruitfulness,
> Close bosom-friend of the maturing sun;

conspiring with him how to load and bless
with fruit the vines that round the thatch-eves run;
To bend with apples the moss'd cottage-trees,
And fill all fruit with ripeness to the core.

Keats may have lived a relatively short life, but his legacy to the artists who followed him (in all fields) is worthy of mention. Keats was a formative influence on Webb, Tennyson, T.S. Eliot, Yeats, Lawrence, and Hardy to name a few. His poetry was also immortalised in the artwork of the Pre-Raphaelite brotherhood, who painted works based on many of his poems, such as 'La Belle Dame Sans Merci', 'Isabella' and 'The Eve of Saint Agnes'. For such a young life, the ripples through the pond left by his passing went wide.

Mary Webb (1881 – 1928)

In 1928, Stanley Baldwin gave a speech at the Literary Fund dinner in praise of Mary Webb; a little known author who had won the Prix Femina Vie Heureuse for her novel, *Precious Bane*. The following day, The Times ran her obituary: it was five months after she had died at the age of forty six, leaving her sixth novel unfinished.

Soon after, Webb's works received some of the recognition she had so ardently wished for during her lifetime; various biographies were published during the 1930s, but as time passed, this attention waned. Another period of interest came fifty years later which coincided with several events; Gladys Coles published her autobiography of Webb, *Flower of Light* (1978); Virago issued new editions of Webb's novels, and *Precious Bane* was dramatized by the BBC (which is when I first came upon her in my early teens). Although Webb was admired by such illustrious people as Stanley Baldwin, Rebecca West and Walter de la Mare, she is rarely talked about in academic circles, thus Webb remains slightly obscure, and is left out of most canonical lists of writers of her time. While there are fewer than twenty books that are about (or at least have a chapter devoted to) Webb, most are biographical studies, and don't examine Webb's writing in its historical, occult or literary context.

Webb's Life: Putting Her Work in Context

Mary Meredith was born in 1881 in Leighton, Shropshire. Her father, George, had an MA in classics from Oxford, and worked as a private school teacher. He ran a private boys' school from their home, wrote poetry and also kept a home farm. He taught Mary to appreciate literature and nature, taking her out into the local Shropshire countryside and teaching her all the names of the birds, trees and plants. The family moved around quite a lot, but always within the safety of southern Shropshire. Mary's mother, Sarah Alice, was a more complex character. Descended from Sir Walter Scott, Alice had given birth to six children, and spent little time with Mary, whom George had nicknamed his 'Precious Bane', the phrase taken from Milton's *Paradise Lost*. While George taught Mary, and gave her free rein in his library and in the surrounding countryside, Alice engaged a governess, Miss Edith Lory (known as 'Minoni') and she continued Mary's education in the classics. She loved Shakespeare, the Brontes, Milton and Hardy, and developed a strong bond with Minoni. But, at the age of fourteen, she was sent to finishing school in Southport, an experience she did not altogether enjoy. When Mary was sixteen, Alice suffered a riding accident and took to her bed; Mary returned home to help look after the children. She enjoyed playing the maternal role and developed a strong bond with her younger siblings, creating stories, poems and plays to keep them amused. Mary thrived in the absence of her mother.

In the spring of 1900, when Mary was nineteen, her mother made an unexpected reappearance in the family, and threw everything into disarray. She was very Victorian in attitude, and began to clash quite badly with Mary, a pattern that was set to continue for the rest of Mary's life. A year later, Mary became very ill, and developed what would later be recognised as Graves' disease, an incurable illness that was a result of an overactive thyroid. The symptoms were exhaustion, weight loss, nervousness and irritability, a goitre on the neck and slightly protruding eyes. At this stage, the only treatment prescribed by doctors was to spend time in nature. She, in effect, became an invalid for the next two years, and Minoni and George nursed her, and encouraged her to express her thoughts through poetry and in essays. These early thoughts were to be published later in 1917 as the immensely beautiful and detailed poems and essays, entitled *The Spring of Joy*.

Self-conscious about her appearance, Mary threw herself into her writing, but her life was irrevocably altered again in 1909 when her father died. Her intense grief for him and her own continuing ill-health meant she was frail for the next few years, but ventured out into society occasionally, joining a local literary discussion group and attending Cambridge University extension lectures in Shrewsbury. It was at the discussion group that Mary met Henry Webb, a recent graduate of Cambridge, in 1910, and they soon fell in love. They shared a deep love of nature, an interest in literature, and also in matters of the occult. In her book, *Flower of Light*, Mary's principle biographer, Gladys Coles, suggests that Mary had lost any Christian belief she held during her long illness; instead, she found signs of the divine in nature, and sought her noetic experiences there. Henry shared this interest in the more occult side of spirituality, and published his work, *The Silences of the Moon,* in 1911, which became a topic of debate between the couple. This book is extraordinary. It shares the same title as William Butler Yeats's work *Per Amica Silentia Lunae* (published in 1918), the title being taken from *The Aeneid.* For Henry Webb (like Yeats), the book was written as his treatise on his philosophy regarding man's place in nature, and his need to worship aspects of nature instead of religion. In it, he cites all sorts of information that is familiar to the esoteric scholar of today; for example, Cornelius Agrippa's work, which suggests that Henry Webb (and probably Mary) was well versed in esoteric works. Coles states that the book became a topic of long debate for Henry Webb and Mary during their courtship. Sadly, the work has almost completely disappeared through the mists of time, although it is still available online and is worth reading. Henry was never again to publish anything like this, and instead went on to become a teacher, and a writer of dubious success. Nevertheless, the couple married in 1912, and lived many years together very happily.

Mary Webb caused consternation at the wedding, as she chose to invite only the working class people she had befriended on her walks around the local area, and not her own class. This became only one of many battles she fought with her mother over the years, but she was to retain this 'eccentric' approach to society throughout her marriage. She did not quite fit with people of her own leisured class, preferring to grow and sell fruit and vegetables at the local market to supplement the income the couple received from their writing, rather than polite drawing room conversation among lacy doilies. But the country folk too thought her peculiar. One lady I spoke to in Shropshire remembers her mother describing Mary Webb as a 'slightly odd' woman, often seen walking up Lyth Hill to her home from Shrewsbury market chattering away to herself.

For many years, Henry Webb filled the vacuum left by the loss of her father, but Mary had a complex relationship with his mother. A spell spent away living in Weston-Super-Mare led to a period of great homesickness for Mary, and she started to write fiction to recreate the Shropshire landscape that she so missed. The couple soon returned to Shropshire, and both concentrated on their writing. Mary's works were accepted for publication, but she never quite received the attention (or the money) she felt she deserved. Their economic situation was frequently strained, not helped by Mary's inability to hold on to money when she had it. She would frequently buy lavish gifts for the children of the working people she knew, then leaving herself without money for food.

In terms of Webb's historical moment, the First World War and its after-effects were all around her as she wrote: her first novel, *The Golden Arrow,* was published in 1916; *Gone to Earth* (1917) was composed as first reports of experiences in the trenches were becoming known. And yet, somewhat remarkably, Webb never mentions the war in her novels, despite the fact that she had three brothers in the trenches. Andrew Radford, one of the few academics to write about Webb, has suggested that Webb's use of nature writing confronts the horror of the war by offering its curative properties; *The House in Dormer Forest* was published in 1920; *Seven for a Secret* came in 1922; and *Precious Bane* (1924) was written as the ex-servicemen were more visible in London and the devastation of the war was better understood. Additionally, Modernism was in full swing in many of the cities of the world; Webb's contemporaries included West, Joyce, Woolf, Eliot, and Forster, to name only a few. Webb, however, is difficult to pin down in terms of a literary movement. She has never been considered a Modernist, as she flouts those literary conventions in her writing just as she flouted the idea of following convention in her life. She believed that following the crowd, a tenet central to Modernism, made people weak.

As the First World War broke out, Henry Webb managed to evade conscription on the grounds of ill health and the fact that he was one of the few men left to teach boys. With the advance earned by Mary's novel *The House in Dormer Forest*, the couple were able to buy a piece of land on Lyth Hill and build Spring Cottage, the house that Mary described as her 'home of light and colour'. The setting is stunning, giving panoramic views of the Shropshire Hills, and there is a path that walkers can follow to a little wood where Webb used to meditate. When reviews of her book were not good, Mary slipped into depression and doctors recommended a change of scene. The couple moved to London, hoping to improve Mary's growing literary reputation, but London was not quite sure what to make of the eccentric Mary. In London, Webb began to move in literary circles – her work was greatly admired by writers such as Rebecca West, J.M. Barrie, and Walter de la Mare, but she felt slighted by the members of the Bloomsbury set, which included Virginia Woolf, Vita Sackville West and Lytton Strachey. The fact that she made her own clothes did not seem to sit well with fashionable London society.

Eventually, Mary and Henry took a small cottage near Hampstead Heath, returning to Lyth Hill whenever they could.

Mary Webb picked up work writing reviews and articles, while Henry took a teaching post in London, and settled straight in to teaching life, although perhaps a little too far. He developed a very intense (although allegedly platonic) relationship with one of his pupils, Kathleen, and this took him further and further away from his wife. While Mary Webb's literary star was rising, her failing relationship with Henry caused her much distress, particularly when he insisted on bringing Kathleen to Lyth Hill with them. As the distance widened between them, Mary's illness continued to dog her. After a fall in Hampstead, she developed pernicious anaemia; her Graves' disease returned with a vengeance; she became very ill. She spent her last summer alone on Lyth Hill, Henry having emotionally withdrawn from her completely. As her illness became critical, she travelled alone to visit Minoni in St Leonards-on-Sea, near Hastings in East Sussex. There Mary died at the age of forty six, with her last novel unfinished, and her husband absent. Her passing was left mostly unreported, and her plain gravestone in Shrewsbury bears only her name and her dates, with no personal words of love at all.

Webb's death and Henry's subsequent marriage to Kathleen leaves critics with a Ted Hughes-like image of him. Webb's work reached posthumous success in the 1930s and made Henry Webb, and his second wife Kathleen, very wealthy. Demand for Webb's books grew steadily, although she disappeared from view intermittently thereafter.

Some biographies have suggested that it was guilt that led to Henry Webb's own untimely death in 1939 when he 'fell' from the top of Scafell – and it has been suggested this was not the first time he had fallen from a mountain. Sometimes the lives of authors seem more dramatic than fiction, and Webb's is no exception.

Webb and Spirituality

Mary Webb's body of work consists of five completed novels (and one incomplete), a collection of poems, and a number of essays, reviews and short stories. All of them are rich in folklore, nature-descriptions and insight into human character. While some consider her writing to be flowery, those who are drawn to the natural world find her work captivating and truly magical. All of her novels are set in rural Shropshire, and she uses the landscape as if it were a character in its own right. The land is not merely a place to set the stories, it becomes a plot device, a way of building the characters of the novels, and also a way for them to connect to the divine, which is how Nature Mysticism becomes a part of her stories. In life, Webb was often regarded as slightly eccentric. She and her husband had 'dropped out of society' to write and run a cottage garden. Webb would regularly walk the six miles or so across the fields into Shrewsbury to sell flowers and vegetables in the local market. But she also used to spend a lot of time meditating in the outdoors, so much so that field workers would see her in the outdoors as they walked to work, sitting very still. When they returned from the fields at the end of the working day, she would still be in the same spot, barely having moved. It is also said that she would sit for so long that birds would land on her. This was then followed by intense periods of furious writing. By using this method, her first novel was written the space of three weeks.

Part of Webb's love of the outdoors had been instilled in her by her father, who also loved nature, but I also believe that her illness also had a big influence on her. At this time, the treatment prescribed by doctors to patients suffering from the debilitating Graves' disease was to spend quiet time in natural surroundings. Webb developed what Walter de la Mare described as senses that were 'almost microscopic in their delicacy' that meant she could capture the moment in her writing, and Stanley Baldwin wrote that whilst reading her work in Whitehall, one had 'almost the physical sense of being in Shropshire cornfields'. It is this ability to absorb and transport her readers which makes reading Webb such a magical experience, however, Webb adds a further dimension to this. To Webb, nature was not just a 'fortuitous assemblage of pretty things', it was a way of connecting with the divine, and fulfilling two of her perceived three purposes in life, which was for people to love 'his fellow, and nature and the creator of them'. Without this threefold purpose, Webb believed a person was not fully whole. A person who connected to this sense of the divine, would cling 'to the beauty of earth as to a garment, and [s]he feels that the wearer of the garment is God'. This is reminiscent of Phyllis Curott's more contemporary sentiment that, 'Nature makes the divine tangible. Nature is the gown the goddess wears to make herself visible; and the dance the god dances to express his joy. Looking at Nature, we see living, incarnate divinity'.[3]

While it would be very appealing to suggest that Webb was a pagan (or at least a precursor of one), it is never quite that simple; Webb would always resist labels, and her writing usually defies classification. She also resisted naming her own beliefs. Her biographers believed she rejected Christianity in her late teenage years, but she was not part of any defined group or movement that might enable us to pin-point her. With other authors in this series, it may be possible to state who they were affiliated to, or which groups they identified with, but classifying Webb's own religious affiliations or literary position is like wrestling with water. Webb was largely solitary, and was simply her own person.

To Webb, nature was not only an expression of the divine, and a way of connecting to that presence, but it was also a source of healing. In her 1917 essay, 'Vis Medicatrix Naturae', Webb wrote:

The power of this life, if men will open their hearts to it, will heal them, will create them anew, physically and spiritually. Here is the gospel of the earth, ringing with hope like May mornings with bird-song, fresh and healthy as fields of young grain.

And yet this connection was not confined to those living in a rural idyll; Webb believed that nothing should prevent a person from connecting with nature, even in the city. She expressed similar sentiments to pagans today, who (like me) maintain an active nature-based path whilst still living in towns and cities. To Webb, nature was accessible through the smallest window box, or the animals and birds around us. She said, 'a single violet can be as effective as an acre of them for finding the way into the land of God'. It was in this minuteness of detail that she observed: leaves unfurling, birds flying, and the white clover falling asleep in the meadows. It was this detail that then translated into her written work, both her poetry and her fiction.

Nature was also a purifier, and a cleansing influence. Webb believed the most spiritual of experiences was fragrance, and that:

The whole earth is a thurible heaped with incense, afire with the divine, yet not consumed. This is the most spiritual of earth's joys... If we washed our souls in the healing perfumes as often as we wash our hands, our lives would be infinitely more wholesome.

And yet Webb was familiar with the shadow side of life; the loss of her father had a profound influence on her, and her own sickness and resulting facial disfigurement meant she lived with pain, but she found her consolation in the 'flawless forms and colours of nature'.

Webb's Written Work

While Webb started her writing life as a poet, it is as a novelist that most people come to know her. While she wrote five completed novels in total, two of these novels are the most well-known; *Gone to Earth* and *Precious Bane*, and yet the lesser known novels, *The Golden Arrow, Seven for a Secret* and *The House in*

Dormer Forest are worth looking at too. For a woman of her time, Webb expressed some quite extraordinary ideas that caused some consternation in her home county, and led to a few book burning incidents. For instance, her lead character, Deborah, in *The Golden Arrow* moves in to live with her lover outside of wedlock, which was obviously too shocking for some of her readers at the time.

Similarly, her heroine, Hazel Woodus, in *Gone to Earth* is somewhat of a free spirit. Hazel is the daughter of a harpist father and a gypsy mother, who abandoned her at an early age as she couldn't bear to be tied down. Hazel then lives with her father, Abel, in a remote part of Shropshire that borders Wales. Her main companion is her pet vixen, Foxy, whom she rescued from a snare. Happier in the company of animals, or enjoying the freedom of the open air, she never really understands the world of humans and 'society'. Sadly, Hazel's idyll does not last, when her father threatens to kill Foxy if she kills another chicken, Hazel vows to marry the first man who will ask her. To Hazel, Foxy is not good or bad, she is just being a fox, and she can't quite understand why she is judged as bad.

Hazel sat on her heels and thought. It was flight or Foxy. She knew that if she did not take Foxy away, her renewed naughtiness was as certain as sunset.

'You was made bad,' she said sadly but sympathetically. 'Leastways, you wasn't made like watchdogs and house-cats and cows. You was made a fox, and you be a fox, and it's queer-like to me, Foxy, as folk canna see that. They expect you to be what you wanna made to be. You'm made to be a fox; and when you'm busy being a fox they say you'm a sinner!'

In order to help Foxy avoid an unfortunate end by drowning, she enters into a 'triangle amoureux' with two men: the local preacher Edward Marsden, who lives with his rather hysterical mother on 'God's Little Mountain', and Reddin the local squire, who lives a selfish existence of hunting, horse-breeding and philandering at Undern Hall. It is Edward that Hazel marries, but she finds herself inextricably drawn to Reddin's more animalistic nature, despite the fact that she is against everything he stands for – particularly hunting. But the child-like Hazel's tragedy is that neither man sees her for what she is. Both want to possess her like an object they can take out and look at when they feel like it, and put her away again in a cupboard when they have other things to do. Like Hardy's *Tess*, Hazel is only ever judged by her outward appearance. Edward sees only her innocence and Reddin sees only her beauty. Reddin eventually lures her away from Edward, rapes her and leaves her pregnant. To relate more of the story would be to give away the ending, but the novel has some themes that still remain as pertinent today, and probably have wider appeal now than they would have had in 1917. Webb was clearly opposed to hunting, and indeed cruelty in any form, as was demonstrated by her lifelong vegetarianism. In one scene, Hazel visits the local town with Edward's mother, and is horrified to see a painting of the crucifixion in one of the shops. To Hazel, how anyone can glorify cruelty to another person is beyond her, whether it is in the name of religion or not.

'What is it, my dear?' Mrs. Marston looked over her spectacles, and her eyes were like half-moons peering over full moons.

'That there picture! They'm hurting Him so cruel. And Him fast and all.'

'Oh!' said Mrs. Marston wonderingly, 'that's nothing to get vexed about. Why, don't you know that's Jesus Christ dying for us?'

'Not for me!' flashed Hazel.

'My dear!'

'No. What for should He? There shall none die along of me, much less be tormented.'

'Needs be that one Man die for the people,' quoted Mrs. Marston easily. 'Only through blood can sin be washed white.'

'Blood makes things raddled, not white; and if so be any's got to die, I'll die for myself.'

To her Christian mother-in-law, this is clearly blasphemous, but Hazel sees no difference between the cruelty shown to a rabbit caught in a snare and the barbarity of one human to another. The views expressed in the book probably have more in common with contemporary ideas regarding ecology, while the constant sanguinary imagery throughout the book suggests to me that this is how the horror of the First World War emerges in Webb's work.

Webb's last completed novel, and possibly her most well-rounded one, was *Precious Bane*. It is the story of Prue Sarn and her family, who live at the very atmospheric Sarn Mere in northern Shropshire. The mere is described as an enchanted place, thrice ringed by trees, reeds and water lilies:

So the mere was three times ringed about, as if it had been three times put in a spell. First there was the ring of oaks and larches, willows, ollern trees and beeches, solemn and strong, to keep the world out. Then there was the ring of rushes, sighing thinly, brittle and sparse, but enough, with their long, trembling shadows, to keep the spells in.

Webb weaves a spell in the landscape, transporting us into a numinous landscape where anything can happen. But the mere is also liminal, a magical circle, a space between the worlds. This is an intensely feminine landscape, ruled by the elements of water and earth, where creation and transformation are part of the turning wheel of the year. Added to this, the land around Sarn is said to be constantly dripping in water, and is often surrounded by mist that brings forth ghosts and apparitions from the past.

The mere is also steeped in folklore, evoking drowned worlds that have been swallowed by its waters, with folktales of a ghostly village that lies at the bottom of the lake, and a church whose bell still tolls across the water on Sundays. Prue has been blighted since birth owing to (according to local belief) her mother being cursed by a crossing hare when she was pregnant, and Prue's resulting hare lip means that she is expected never to marry. There is a clear correlation here to the connection in folklore between witches and hares, and Prue's story is no exception. The local country folk believe that the outer face must represent what lies inside, and so whispers of 'witch' follow Prue wherever she goes.

They'd reasoned it out slow, as we do in the country, but once they came to the end of the reasoning they were fixed, and it would take a deal to turn them. This was the reason for the hating looks, the turnings aside, the whispers. I was the witch of Sarn. I was the woman cursed of God with a hare-shotten lip. I was the woman who had friended Beguildy, that wicked old man, the devil's oddman, and like holds to like. And now, almost the worst crime of all, I stood alone.

Prue's outward disfigurement makes her officially unmarriageable, so her brother sends her to the local cunning man, Beguildy, to be educated. This only further compounds her cursed nature with the local population, as she is now consorting with the local wizard, the devil's man. Although Webb refers to Beguildy as a wizard, this is no Gandalf of fantasy fiction.

For a wizard could not rightly be called a servant of His, but one of Lucifer's men. Not that Beguildy was wicked, but only empty of good, as if all the righteousness was burnt out by the flame of his fiery mind, which must know and intermeddle with mysteries. As for love, he did not know the word. He could read the stars, and tell the future, and he claimed to have laid spirits. Once I asked him where the future was, that he could see it so plain. And he said, 'It lies with the past, child, at the back of Time.' You couldn't ever get the better of Mister Beguildy.

Beguildy has a heart that does not know love, but (as his name suggests) he has the mental agility to twist words and beguile most of the country people around him. *Precious Bane* contains one of the few authentic portrayals of a cunning man in literature. The Wizard Beguildy is worthy of any of Owen Davies' descriptions of the real thing in history, from his dubious magical powers, to his outlandish wardrobe, right down to the half-house-half-cave that he lives in. Beguildy is someone who stands on the edge of the civilisation, consorting with spirits and the darker side of creation that most country folk are too afraid to confront. Not only that, but the entire plot of the novel turns on a curse he lays on Prue's brother, Gideon Sarn, to die by fire and water.

Beguildy is not only able to lay spirits, bless, heal and curse, but he also has an elaborate 'ritual' he performs for the wealthiest of men in which he 'raises Venus' in his home. For a small fee, the men can sit in his parlour and watch as the goddess herself ascends into the room, presumably from the underworld (or in this case, Beguildy's cellar) while Beguildy chants the spell in a room filled with incense and the rosy glow of lamp light. The men are unaware that Venus herself is in fact Prue, taking the place of Beguildy's beautiful daughter, standing naked on a pulley system, her imperfect face veiled in muslin. For one evening, this ritual allows her to take the place of the most desired and beautiful goddess, away from the stigma of her disfigurement. This ritual, at least, unknowingly acknowledges the divine in her.

And as I saw the squire's shoulders stooped forrard with the weight of his longing I knew for the first time that, whatever my face might be, my body was fair enough. From foot to shoulder I was as passable as any woman could be. Under the red light my flesh was like rose petals, and the shape of me was such as the water-fairies were said to have, lissom and lovesome.

For an essentially non-pagan writer (since Modern Paganism was not to emerge until several decades later) Webb is remarkably pagan. She has a good grasp of the traditional associations with Venus (both the goddess and the planet) that are ascribed by occult theorists and practitioners such as Agrippa, which Webb was probably familiar with. Since Webb's own husband makes reference to Agrippa (among others) in *The Silences of the Moon*, it is highly likely that Webb herself was also familiar with the *Three Books of Occult Philosophy* which ascribes different planetary associations to colours, plants and stones. Venus is desired, her 'body is fair', she is seen 'under red light', with 'flesh like rose petals', and her shape is 'such as the water fairies were said to have' in line with Venus' birth from the sea. Venus and Prue are both 'lissom and lovesome'. What other occult texts Webb may have been familiar with, we will never know. Webb kept no diaries, and at her death, Henry Webb destroyed most of her correspondence and possessions, including the little library of books she had collected.

Precious Bane is also awash with references to folklore, from the folk songs the children sing, such as 'Green Gravel', to the references to local traditions such as love spinning, the Wild Hunt, and sin eating. When her violent father dies suddenly in a fit of rage, the family cannot afford to pay a sin eater, the practice where someone was paid to consume something which sympathetically represented the deceased person's sins. This meant they could freely enter heaven, being now 'sin free'. Prue's

brother Gideon strikes a bargain with their mother: in return for
his acting as sin eater for his father, she must turn the farm over
to him. His plan is to work hard, enlisting the help of Prue, earn
as much money as they can so that Prue can try to be cured, and
he can buy a large house and live the life of a wealthy man. As his
plan consumes every bit of his strength and Prue's, it is his all-
consuming love of money that becomes his precious bane, while
Prue's pureness of heart and love of the weaver eventually sees
her safely into a better life.

The love story between Prue and Kester the weaver is both
believable and compelling, since Kester sees beyond outside
appearances alone. Added to this, Webb's familiar style of nature
descriptions both enable Prue to escape from the drudgery of her
life, and also connect to the divine through nature. The character
of Prue then, is herself a Nature Mystic, as she connects to the
divine in the quiet places, such as the attic, where she tucks
herself away to write. In the quiet of this place, surrounded by
the bountiful harvest of apples, she has her first numinous
encounter. Prue cannot quite describe the noetic force she has
encountered, but she knows it is a force of the natural world, and
not one evoked in a traditional religious setting.

And even now, when Parson says, 'It was the power of the
Lord working in you,' I'm not sure in my own mind. For there
was naught in it of churches nor of folks, praying nor praising,
sinning nor repenting. It had to do with such things as bird-
song and daffadowndillies rustling, knocking their heads
together in the wind. And it was as wilful in its coming and
going as a breeze over the standing corn. It was a queer thing,
too, that a woman who spent her days in sacking, cleaning
sties and beast-housen, living hard, considering over fardens,
should come of a sudden into such a marvel as this. For
though it was so quiet, it was a great miracle, and it changed
my life; for when I was lost for something to turn to, I'd run to

the attic, and it was a core of sweetness in much bitter. Though the visitation came but seldom, the taste of it was in the attic all the while. I had but to creep in there, and hear the bees making their murmur, and smell the woody o'er-sweet scent of kept apples, and hear the leaves rasping softly on the window-frame, and watch the twisted grey twigs on the sky, and I'd remember it and forget all else.

It is not difficult to see why *Precious Bane* would appeal to someone on a pagan path, since it contains many of the elements that Ronald Hutton and others have ascribed to the development of Modern Paganism. The atmosphere of the story is dripping with references to folk magic and folklore. Prue's appeal as the narrator of the story also draws the reader in, since the first person narrative enables us to see the action directly through her eyes, and because of this we never truly get to see Prue's disfigurement. We feel the love, loss, longing and isolation she feels living outside of her own society, being touted as the outsider who must be feared and persecuted, but the reader only engages with the inner nature of Prue, since here is no narrator outside of her. This places the reader at the heart of the local superstition, tradition and magic, all elements familiar to those drawn to Modern Paganism.

If your path is one that involves close work with nature and following the wheel of the year, then I would defy you to not to be captivated by Prue and Kester's story, as I was, long before I really understood the significance of what I was reading. *Precious Bane* remains one of those books I re-visit from year to year, and each time I read it, I never fail to fall under its spell. Just why Webb has failed to gain the recognition she deserves is not clear. While some may find her descriptions flowery, her sense of poetry comes through even in her fiction, and her descriptions of nature are undoubtedly beautiful. It is possible that it is in her ability to evade classification that she slips through the net. Whatever the reason, her work is a rare blossom waiting to be discovered.

Thomas Hardy (1840 – 1928)

'Happiness is but a mere episode in the general drama of pain,' wrote Thomas Hardy in *The Mayor of Casterbridge*. This probably sums up what most people think of Hardy's works, born from the much wailing and gnashing of teeth that often come from studying the books at school. Invariably in Hardy, there is love found and rapidly lost, high-feeling characters that are misunderstood, and characters who lose the fight against their circumstances in life. There is also a heavy sense of death and tragedy, but the counterweight to this is Hardy's observation of character, his compelling story lines, and his absolute love of the land. Hardy also said: 'The business of the poet and the novelist is to show the sorriness underlying the grandest things and the grandeur underlying the sorriest things.' Thus, his novels offer a social commentary of the period that can easily be overlooked. I have chosen two of Hardy's novels which, I believe, exemplify this quality and also capture elements that will appeal to twenty-first century pagans: *The Return of the Native* and *Tess of the D'Urbervilles*.

Hardy's Life: Putting His Work in Context

Thomas Hardy's life spanned two centuries that were poles apart in terms of social attitudes and zeitgeist. Born in 1840 in Higher Bockhampton near Dorchester, Hardy's father was a stonemason, and his mother (who was very well read) educated him at home until he was eight. The young Hardy was then sent to a local school where his education continued until he was sixteen years old. At sixteen, Hardy's formal education ended, since his family did not have the means to pay for continuing studies at a university. Hardy was then apprenticed to a local architect, which became his trade.

In 1862, Hardy moved to London, where he was able to enrol

at King's College and study architecture further. He was a very successful architect, winning prizes for his work, but he struggled to settle in London. Noticing the distinct class differences that were even more pronounced than in his rural Dorset, and living right by the Thames, took its toll on Hardy; five years later he returned to Dorset struggling with ill health. Once there, Hardy continued to work as an architect, but he also began to take his writing more seriously. He had always written poems and considered himself a poet, but he now began to write novels as well. Hardy's first novel, *The Poor Man and the Lady,* failed to find a publisher, and he later destroyed the manuscript. His second and third novels, *Desperate Remedies* and *Under the Greenwood Tree,* were more successful. When he published *Far From the Madding Crowd* in 1874, the book was so successful that it enabled him to give up his career in architecture to focus on writing. It also enabled him to marry his first wife, Emma, whom he had met and fallen in love with whilst working on a church restoration project in Cornwall.

The success of Hardy's marriage to Emma was mootable; the couple quickly fell out of love, and later became estranged. Hardy's novels frequently feature stories of love gone wrong, and couples who fall rapidly in love, marry, then find they have been deceived (or have deceived themselves) in the throes of passion, and are left to deal with the consequences. It is highly likely these recurring story lines reflect Hardy's own experience. And yet, when Emma died in 1912, Hardy was overcome with remorse, and went on to produce what critics say was his finest poetry. In 1914, despite his continuing preoccupation with Emma's death, Hardy married his secretary, Florence, who was thirty nine years his junior. He continued to idolise Emma for the rest of his life.

Despite the fact that his books had attracted controversy (*Jude the Obscure* was famously burnt by a bishop, and the themes of unmarried motherhood and sex in *Tess* also caused outrage) in his later years, Hardy became quite a grand old man amongst writers. Mary Webb dedicated *Gone to Earth* to Hardy; D.H. Lawrence was also notably influenced by Hardy, as were Virginia Woolf, T.E. Lawrence, Mary Butts, Siegfried Sassoon, and Robert Graves – author of the Modern Pagan's canonical text, *The White Goddess*.

Thomas Hardy died in January 1928, and had one of the most aberrant burials in literary history. Hardy's wish was to be buried with his first wife Emma in Dorset, but his estate's executors were adamant he should be buried in Westminster Abbey. As a compromise, his heart was removed from his body and buried with Emma, while his ashes were interred next to Charles Dickens in Poets' Corner.

Hardy and Spirituality

Hardy is another writer whose personal belief systems are not all that easy to pin down to a straightforward classification. His family was Anglican, and regularly attended church. His father's passion was music, and he contributed to music in the church, along with Hardy's uncle. As a young man, Hardy was said to have dabbled with conversion to the Plymouth Brethren, the conservative Evangelical movement into which Aleister Crowley was born. Hardy later decided against conversion, and began to question traditional Christianity and its view of god. Ultimately, he rejected Christianity and followed his own path, which incorporated ideas of deism (the belief that the observation of the natural world is enough to justify a belief in god), and Spiritism (similar to Spiritualism, except that Spiritism is not considered a religious sect, but more a philosophy or way of life). To these was added agnosticism, yet Hardy was clearly interested in spirituality. He frequently expressed ideas about the nature of the power that controls the universe in his work. He also expressed many ideas about the divine qualities found in humans. Of Tess, Hardy wrote the following:

She knew how to hit to a hair's breadth that moment of evening when the light and the darkness are so evenly balanced that the constraint of day and the suspense of night neutralize each other, leaving absolute mental liberty... At times her whimsical fancy would intensify natural processes around her till they seemed a part of her own story. Rather they became a part of it; for the world is only a psychological phenomenon, and what they seemed, they were. The midnight airs and gusts, moaning amongst the tightly wrapped buds and bark of the winter twigs, were formulae of bitter reproach. A wet day was the expression of irremediable grief at her weakness in the mind of some vague ethical being whom she could not class definitely as the God of her childhood, and could not comprehend as any other.

Tess too, then, is a Nature Mystic, since she sees the emotional detail of her own life reflected back in the details of the seasons, as if she can change nature around her with some form of natural witchcraft. (The 'wet day was the expression of irremediable grief' while the moaning of the wind is the god's way of giving her a 'bitter reproach'). The idea of the world only being a 'psychological phenomenon' and not 'real' seems a remarkably modern concept for Hardy's time. There is also a strong sense of animism in Hardy's descriptions of nature and the universe, and his characters often interact with the world with a strong sense of there being a powerful force that controls events, but it is inexpressible. In a letter to a clergyman, Hardy once described this ineffable being as 'a new concept of universal consciousness' or the 'unconscious will of the universe', which he hoped was sympathetic.

Hardy's Written Work

Hardy is often compared to that other Victorian social commentator, Charles Dickens; they had much in common in terms of their style and themes, favouring the realist style of writing. However, there is one obvious difference: while Dickens was essentially urban, and frequently centred his stories on London, Hardy's novels are almost always rural. Even the towns featured are the provincial ones, and do not contain the harsher urbanisation of the metropolis. In particular, Hardy is synonymous with his portrayal of 'Wessex', based on the medieval Anglo-Saxon kingdom. Wessex was based on parts of Dorset, Wiltshire, Somerset, Devon, Berkshire and Hampshire. Like Dickens, Hardy's work was often originally serialised in magazines; one of his stories *A Pair of Blue Eyes*, is thought to be what inspired the term 'cliff-hanger' as one of his characters was literally left hanging from a cliff at the end of an episode. Hardy was a prolific writer throughout his lifetime, producing numerous novels, volumes of poetry, short stories and dramas. *The Return of the Native* (first published in 1878) and *Tess of the D'Urbervilles* (first published in 1891) are considered 'mature' works; that is, Hardy was writing full time by then, and they are very typical of his style of writing.

The Return of the Native is possibly less well known than *Tess*, which is more commonly found on reading lists, but it is a beautiful novel, set in a stunning landscape. At the time of writing, Hardy had problems finding a publisher because of the themes of the novel, and so it was published in a serialised format in Belgravia magazine. The novel takes place on the fictional Egdon Heath, which was based on the heath where Hardy grew up, and the landscape (and how it functions) becomes a vital part of the novel. The events of the novel take place over a year and a day, a familiar timespan in both folk tradition and Modern Paganism since traditional handfastings were intended to last for a year and a day to begin with, and training circles refer to the preparation period for initiation as the 'year and a day'.

At the opening of the novel, Diggory Venn drives across the heath in his wagon, with a hidden female passenger in the back. The woman is Thomasin Yeobright, who is in some distress.

Thomasin had left her home to elope with Damon Wildeve, a local innkeeper, but events have conspired to prevent the marriage from taking place. Thomasin, then, is returning home in disgrace, and is unsure if the marriage will ever take place. Venn is known throughout the novel as 'The Reddleman', on account of his trade: he sells 'reddle', or red ochre, to farmers to mark their sheep, but this leaves him dyed red from head to foot. Venn stands outside of society, and is somewhat of an outcast on account of this appearance, but it also marks him out and enables him to observe events in a way that no one 'on the inside' could. Thomasin and Venn have a history; he had proposed to her several years before, but was turned down. What Thomasin doesn't know is that Diggory has remained in love with her ever since; his loyalty has never wavered. However, he knows his trade and his appearance will leave him with no chance of winning her affections. Venn is the antithesis of Wildeve, who is a rough, selfish man, easily bored and extremely fickle. Underneath his red-stained demonic appearance, Venn is kind, shrewd, and very wise. Thomasin returns to her aunt, Mrs Yeobright, and they agree that Wildeve must be made to marry Thomasin, as her reputation will be ruined for running away with him and returning unmarried. But Wildeve has other priorities; he is still pre-occupied with his previous love, the beautiful but volatile Eustacia Vye. Eustacia loathes Egdon Heath and longs to escape to somewhere more exciting. Eustacia roams the heath each day, and the local inhabitants are certain she is a witch. She too is fickle, wanting only what she cannot have. Her relationship with Wildeve was only attractive to her as there were no other alternatives:

To be loved to madness – such was her great desire. Love was to her the one cordial which could drive away the eating loneliness of her days. And she seemed to long for the abstraction called passionate love more than for any particular lover.

Eustacia is clearly more in love with the idea of being in love, than with the real love of any particular man. Hardy describes Eustacia as being like a goddess, albeit an imperfect one:

> Eustacia Vye was the raw material of a divinity. On Olympus she would have done well with a little preparation. She had the passions and instincts which make a model goddess, that is, those which make not quite a model woman. Had it been possible for the earth and mankind to be entirely in her grasp for a while, she had handled the distaff, the spindle, and the shears at her own free will, few in the world would have noticed the change of government. There would have been the same inequality of lot, the same heaping up of favours here, of contumely there, the same generosity before justice, the same perpetual dilemmas, the same captious alteration of caresses and blows that we endure now.

This short piece not only reveals Eustacia's character, but also something of Hardy's attitude to divinity – that it is not perfect, and is subject to the same whims and capriciousness that mortals are subject to. It is not the remote, withdrawn deity of the church, but rather something that lives and breathes and walks amongst us. Divinity spins the web of creation, holding the 'distaff, the spindle, and the shears' and it does so at its own free will. Divinity is not guided by rules or fairness, it is fickle and unfair.

When Thomasin's cousin, Clym Yeobright, returns from Paris, events are further thrown into disarray. Although Clym's intention is to establish a school for the children of the poor local heath dwellers, Eustacia quickly fixates on him as a way of escaping Egdon, and travelling to somewhere more exotic. She believes that if she marries him, they will go to Paris or some other far-flown destination. Eustacia and Clym rapidly fall in love and marry (much to the distress of his mother, Mrs Yeobright), but soon after Eustacia discovers her error, when

Clym informs her of his intention to remain on Egdon Heath. Realising that he has finally lost Eustacia, Wildeve finally marries Thomasin, and Hardy's usual portrayal of the disappointed marriage that cannot be escaped comes into play. Both couples find little happiness in their marriages. Clym spends long hours studying, and becomes very ill, losing his sight for some time. This means he is unable to take up teaching, and instead becomes a furze cutter in order to support himself and Eustacia; this is the final humiliation for her: living on the heath in a lowly hut, and married to a labourer. She looks for an escape. Meanwhile Wildeve tires of Thomasin, and becomes infatuated once more with Eustacia – to both of their dooms.

While Eustacia as a heroine is imperfect and frequently unlikeable, Tess, by contrast represents everything that is good, but also all that is unfair in the world. Similar to Mary Webb's Hazel in *Gone to Earth*, Tess represents the innocence and purity to be found in nature, and how the harshness of life (and mankind) can be its undoing. Tess is born into a poor rural family, the Durbeyfields. Her mother is kind but distracted and foolish, and her father is a drinker. Mr Durbeyfield is told by a neighbour that he is in fact distantly related to the D'Urbervilles, a wealthy family. What Durbeyfield doesn't know is that the D'Urbervilles are an extinct family line, and their title and lands were bought by another family who are of no relation. When the family experiences yet another financial setback, Tess is dispatched to visit the D'Urbervilles to claim kinship and see if they will help, but this triggers a sequence of events that lead to Tess's downfall. On finding the D'Urbervilles, Tess meets Alec D'Urberville, a self-absorbed, spoilt rake, who rapes her. Tess she is left pregnant and alone. She returns to her mother's house and has the child (whom she names Sorrow), but he is a sickly thing, and dies soon after. Tess leaves and finds work on a dairy farm, where she meets Angel Clare, the son of a wealthy family who wants to make his own way in life as a farmer. He falls in love with Tess, believing her to be pure, and perfect farmer's wife material, and for a time their love is perfect, but only because Angel does not look for the real Tess, just his perfect image of her:

> There was hardly a touch of earth in her love for Clare. To her sublime trustfulness he was all that goodness could be – knew all that a guide, philosopher, and friend should know. She thought every line in the contour of his person the perfection of masculine beauty, his soul the soul of a saint, his intellect that of a seer. The wisdom of her love for him, as love, sustained her dignity; she seemed to be wearing a crown. The compassion of his love for her, as she saw it, made her lift up her heart to him in devotion. He would sometimes catch her large, worshipful eyes, that had no bottom to them looking at him from their depths, as if she saw something immortal before her.

Unable to tell Angel the truth about her past, Tess marries him, but on their wedding night she finally finds the courage to reveal her secret, believing she is safe in the knowledge that he loves her, so he will forgive her. His illusions are shattered and, unable to reconcile the real Tess with his fantasy of her, he rejects her and goes overseas. Tess's fortunes grow worse and worse, until she feels the entire cosmos to be against her:

> 'Did you say the stars were worlds, Tess?'
> 'Yes.'
> 'All like ours?'
> 'I don't know, but I think so. They sometimes seem to be like the apples on our stubbard-tree. Most of them splendid and sound – a few blighted.'
> 'Which do we live on – a splendid one or a blighted one?'
> 'A blighted one.'

Although Tess writes to Angel and begs him to return and help her, he is very sick and unable to come. Unlucky Tess falls back into the clutches of Alec D'Urberville. After months of persistent chasing on Alec's part, and with no other option for survival due to the death of her father, Tess is compelled to become Alec's mistress in order to safeguard her family's future. Angel returns to England, having decided he must reclaim Tess, but he is too late. In desperation, Tess tells Angel to leave, then kills Alec and flees with Angel. The novel reaches its climax in the infamous scene at Stonehenge, where, shrouded in mist, Tess lies on the altar to sleep, like a sacrifice to the gods. She awakes to find they are surrounded by their pursuers and cannot escape.

Tess dies on the hangman's rope. She, like Webb's Hazel, has an innocence that can only lead to her downfall when she must live amongst men. There is a fatalistic inevitability to her demise, resulting from the apparent folly of those around her. Like Hazel, the men in Tess's life do not see her for her real self, only the constructed image of what they want her to be, and they are too caught up in their own dramas to protect her. To Alec, she is a sweet conquest, while to Angel she is a perfect 'statue' of a woman, which does not allow her to have thoughts, feelings or needs of her own.

Tess of the D'Urbervilles was a great inspiration to many writers and artists. Although Tess, like many well-known works, can suffer by being too well known in popular culture, the novel is well worth re-assessing. Hardy's descriptions of the Wessex countryside, and his perception of human behaviour, make the book well rounded and very appealing. At first glance, Tess herself may appear to be weak and not worthy of being a modern heroine, but she has an inner strength, resourcefulness and self-determination that underlies the tragedy of her circumstances. And she is also a useful lesson in the brevity and fragility of human life, and in not taking the opinions of others too seriously:

She might have seen that what had bowed her head so profoundly – the thought of the world's concern at her situation – was founded on illusion. She was not an existence, an experience, a passion, a structure of sensations, to anybody but herself. To all humankind besides, Tess was only a passing thought.

Sylvia Townsend Warner (1893 – 1978)

To describe Sylvia Townsend Warner as a rebel would be an understatement. While all of the male writers will be familiar, some of our women writers have been forgotten over time. All of the previously forgotten women writers in this series show extraordinary character and brilliance in their own unique ways, and each of them deserves to be rediscovered for their own quality of writing, as much as for their uncommon character. Sylvia Townsend Warner was a trailblazer of the best kind, and she turned the view of women in the inter-war period on its head, particularly the view of unmarried and lesbian women. For a writer who has been so singularly ignored by critics and academics alike until very recently, Townsend Warner's writing career was very enduring; she was actively writing and being published between 1925 and 1978, and spent forty years contributing stories and articles to *The New York Times*. Her oeuvre, then, is long and varied, and worthy of greater exploration. It is entirely possible that it was her political stance and her alternative lifestyle that set her apart from the literary world, and left her to be disregarded for so many years. Whatever the reason, Townsend Warner wrote witty and irreverent stories that are well worth exploring, and she deserves more credit than she has been given.

Townsend Warner's Life: Putting Her Work in Context

Sylvia Townsend Warner was born in December 1893, the daughter of a Harrow housemaster and a mother with whom she never really saw eye to eye. Townsend Warner's father died when she was nine years old, and so she was sent away to live in Devon. Although her upbringing in Devon was a happy one, she was badly affected by the death of her father. When the First World War broke out in 1914, Townsend Warner moved to

London to work in a munitions factory, which was unusual for a woman of her age and class at that time. During the 1920s, she knew and associated with a number of the 'Bright Young Things' in London, a group of aristocratic young people who experimented with drugs, drank copious amounts of alcohol and threw lavish parties. The group included Cecil Beaton, Evelyn Waugh, Edith Sitwell and Nancy Mitford, and were immortalised in Waugh's book *Vile Bodies*. Townsend Warner's lifestyle defied convention from an early age; not only did she work in the munitions factory, but from the age of nineteen, she also had a long standing affair with a much older married man. In 1923 she met T.F. Powys, whose work she encouraged, and he in turn encouraged her writing career. Her first novel was published in 1926, and in 1930, at the age of thirty four, she met the person who would change her life forever. Valentine Ackland was a poet; the two women fell in love, and moved to rural Dorset.

Ackland herself was quite a complex character. Born Mary Kathleen Ackland, 'Molly' as she was known, came from a wealthy background, but in her family, time and attention were substituted for material wealth; rather than spend time with their children, Ackland's parents instead spent money on them, and neglected their emotional needs. Bullied by her older sister, and when she did see her father, he moulded her into a symbolic son, teaching her shooting and boxing. Ackland was brought up in a Catholic household, and at nineteen had married Richard Turpin, a gay man who was unable to consummate the marriage. Less than a year later, their marriage was annulled. By the time she met Townsend Warner in 1930, Molly had become well aware of the gender bias in society, had changed her name to the more androgynous Valentine, and started dressing in men's clothing. Ackland was a poet, and published a volume of poems with Townsend Warner, *Whether a Dove or a Seagull*, as well as several volumes of confessional poetry and memoirs. Although Ackland and Townsend Warner stayed together for many years, the relationship was troubled; Ackland was crippled with self-doubt and alcoholism, and was not faithful to Townsend Warner. For several years she led parallel relationships with Townsend Warner and the American heiress, Elizabeth Wade Wright. She also had doubts about her own gender identity, and her own religious affiliation. Ackland at first rejected the Catholicism of her upbringing, and looked to the Quaker faith for answers, but then returned to Catholicism towards the end of her life, which gave Townsend Warner some discomfort. Despite the tumultuous nature of their relationship, Ackland and Townsend Warner had stayed together until Ackland's death from breast cancer in 1969, some thirty nine years. Townsend Warner survived Ackland by a further nine years, until she too passed away in May 1978.

What sets both Ackland and Townsend Warner apart from other contemporaries is their political stance. Not only were they openly lesbian and living together in what can only be described as a marriage in all but name, but they were also outwardly political. Ackland involved Townsend Warner in membership of the Communist Party in the 1930s, and they both spent time in Spain during the Spanish Civil War. Both women came under investigation by MI5 for their involvement with the Communist Party. Townsend Warner did not remain a member of the Communist Party for her whole life, but she did retain her political activities and interests.

Townsend Warner's Written Work

Townsend Warner's most well-known novel is *Lolly Willowes or The Gentle Huntsman*, which was published in 1926. Laura Willowes is a young woman who, much to the chagrin of her family, remains unmarried. She lives with her parents at the family home, Lady Place, where she prefers to grow and gather herbs, and brew beer. But life cannot remain unchanging, and with the death of her father, she is packed off to live in London with her brother and his family. Finding life as Maiden Aunt Lolly unfulfilling, she decides to take her life into her own hands, and moves to the country, to live in a village called Great Mop. Once she settles in to independent life in the country, Lolly spends her time exploring the local countryside, and getting to know the rather curious inhabitants of Great Mop, who all seem to mysteriously disappear into the countryside once a month. Lolly soon discovers that the villagers are in fact a coven of witches, who dance ecstatically under the stars with their leader, the devil. Invited to join them, Lolly takes an oath to the devil and becomes a witch, gathering about her the remaining accoutrements that go with that role; she lives in a cottage in the countryside and has previously practiced herb crafts, but now she also adopts her familiar, a black cat she calls Vinegar.

But life as a witch is not immediately straightforward. Lolly feels as socially awkward at the Witches' Sabbath as she had at social events and parties:

> A familiar discouragement began to settle upon her spirits. In spite of her hopes she was not going to enjoy herself. Even as a witch, it seemed, she was doomed to social failure, and her first Sabbath was not going to open livelier vistas than were opened by her first ball. She remembered her dancing days in Somerset, Hunt Balls and County Balls in the draughty Assembly Rooms. With the best intentions she had never managed to enjoy them. The first hour was well enough, but after that came increasing listlessness and boredom.

Telling Satan that she does not like the Sabbath one bit, she walks off into the night. Not knowing where she is in the dark, she decides to wait until dawn comes before returning home, and as daylight comes, she finds herself on the edge of a wood. Out of the trees comes striding a gamekeeper, who talks with Lolly in a kind way, and asks her if she will remain in Great Mop, as it would be a shame for her to leave now. Lolly realises that she has nowhere else to go, and the gentle huntsman tells her that he will always be there to help her. All she need do is seek for him in the woods, and ask for assistance, and he will be by her side:

'I hope you will stay here, Miss Willowes.'

She spoke a little sadly. In this unaccustomed hour her soul was full of doubts. She wondered if, having flouted the Sabbath, she were still a witch, or whether, her power being taken from her... And being faint for want of food and want of sleep, she foreboded the worst.

'Yes, you must stay here. It would be a pity to go now.'

Laura nearly said, 'I have nowhere to go,' but a dread of exile came over her like a salt wave, and she could not trust herself to speak to this kind man. He came nearer and said:

'Remember, Miss Willowes, that I shall always be very glad to help you. You have only to ask me.'

'But where shall I find you?' she asked, too much impressed by the kindness of his words to think him strange.

'You will always find me in the wood,' he answered, and touching his cap he walked away. She heard the noise of swishing branches and the scuff of feet among dead leaves growing fainter as he went further into the wood.

Lolly Willowes is a novel that can be read on several different levels. While at face value it is a story about a woman who makes a pact with the devil and becomes a witch, there are also many layers underneath this, which make the novel ahead of its time. During the interwar years, a woman's worth was very much tied to her marital status, and spinsters were viewed as being unfulfilled. A whole generation of young men had been lost in the Great War, which had left a large number of women unmarried. A large proportion of the female population (an estimated four million women) were viewed (at best) as redundant. Spinsters were viewed as 'hard, dry and unfeminine'. Books instructing readers about a woman's role in marriage stated clearly that the missionary position was the only 'natural' way to engage in sex with one's husband, and a woman's pleasure in her sexual life was not necessary, unless it encouraged her husband and enabled reproduction to occur more easily. Furthermore, women were taught to be afraid of the 'vulgar' and 'man-hating' lesbian seduction, as leading the way to damnation. Women were not expected to take an active part in their own sexuality, least of all to take pleasure from it.

Author and academic Jane Garrity believes that while Lolly's spinsterhood could be read as asexual, it is in fact quite the opposite. For Garrity, Lolly's transformation into a witch serves as a secondary metaphor for her sexuality. There are several points in the novel where Townsend Warner hints at Lolly's emerging sexuality which has previously been stifled, such as when she reaches an ecstatic state while dancing with the red haired village girl at the witches' Sabbath,

Laura liked dancing with Emily; the pasty-faced and anaemic young slattern who she had seen dawdling about the village danced with a fervour that annihilated every misgiving. They whirled faster and faster, fused together like two suns that whirl and blaze in a single destruction. A strand of the red hair came undone and brushed across Laura's face. The contact made her tingle from head to foot. She shut her eyes and dived into obliviousness – with Emily for a partner she could dance until the gunpowder ran out of the heels of her boots.

Also, the devil (who puts in an appearance at the Witches' Sabbath) like Valentine Ackland, is handsomely androgynous in appearance, and Lolly finds this very alluring. Townsend Warner, both in life and in literature, blurred boundaries around what was socially acceptable. For Townsend Warner to openly live with her lover Ackland was shocking at the time, although most of society would have pretended it was not happening, and not acknowledge their role in each other's lives. Added to this, to then publish a novel about a spinster who defied the male members of her family (from father to brothers, and then to nephew) who 'knew best' was curious. When openly lesbian novels like Radcliffe Hall's *The Well of Loneliness* were immediately banned on publication, why was it that *Lolly Willowes* was not? Garrity believes that the novel's style gives the clue as to why it went below the radar of social acceptability. While Townsend Warner did not play with the novel's form (unlike her Modernist contemporaries), *Lolly Willowes* reads like a precursor to the magical realism genre that emerged later in the twentieth century. Although the action is set in a seemingly ordinary society, the magic that emerges in that world sets the events of the novel apart from the 'real world', which meant the novel was largely dismissed by those who found Radcliffe Hall so offensive. And yet the layers that are revealed when reading the novel make it seem ludicrous that it has not been given the attention it deserves before now.

Townsend Warner and Spirituality

As with the other ways of her life, Townsend Warner's spiritual life was equally unconventional. Although Valentine Ackland danced a recurring relationship with the Catholic Church, Townsend Warner rejected Christianity fairly early in adulthood, and never returned to it. While the 1926 publication date of *Lolly Willowes* puts this particular novel long before the public emergence of modern Wicca in the 1950s, or the advent of Modern Paganism, there are some points of comparison in Townsend Warner's own belief system that are of relevance to those following these paths today. These are her interest in witches, especially influenced by the work of Margaret Murray; the subtext of 'hidden knowledge' of hermetic texts and grimoires which pops up in *Lolly Willowes*, and also Townsend Warner's apparent 'topophilia'. Topophilia is the strong sense of identity that comes from the love of a particular place, and is sometimes fused with beliefs of pantheism, or the sacred aspects of nature.

Townsend Warner expressed a deep interest in the 'witches' involved in the witchcraft trials, as she felt drawn to them. She reportedly felt an affinity for those dispossessed by society (probably because of her own marginal position). Garrity reports that Sylvia Townsend Warner had read Margaret Murray's book, *The Witch Cult in Western Europe*, and was very much influenced by it when she wrote *Lolly Willowes*, so much so that when the novel was published, Townsend Warner sent a copy to Margaret Murray. The two women met soon after, and Townsend Warner was so entranced by Murray, that she stated a wish to be part of Margaret Murray's 'coven'. Murray's view (like that of James Frazer's in *The Golden Bough* which was so influential in the early part of the twentieth century) was that witchcraft represented the survival of a Pre-Christian matriarchal nature-worshipping tradition, which was practiced in secret. Although more recent scholars such as Ronald Hutton and Owen Davies have disproved this unbroken link, it was still a very alluring idea, and it provided a more helpful counterpart to the commonly held belief from the Christian tradition that witches worshipped the devil.

Evidence of these beliefs are visible in *Lolly Willowes* (despite Townsend Warner's subversive inclusion of the devil, which is a Christian archetype, and not a pagan one). Aside from Lolly's fondness for brewing and gathering obscure herbs, Lolly also has a tendency to read books that her family and society in general viewed as 'unfeminine' which set all the local ladies into a spin. These included books on philosophy, botany and daemonology, the kinds of books (like Agrippa's *Three Books of Occult Philosophy*) that we now know were read by wise women and cunning men, as explored by Owen Davies. The reading of original grimoires and hermetic texts (as mentioned previously in Keats) often set cunning folk apart from society and enhanced their perceived powers as practitioners of magic. As this was an accepted part of social interactions with practitioners of magic in the late nineteenth and early twentieth centuries, contemporary readers of *Lolly Willowes* may have recognised the significance of this more readily in the subtext of the novel.

Townsend Warner's love of nature and the rural come across in all of her novels. She frequently associates nature with the feminine, while cityscapes become quite masculine and harsher. It is no surprise, therefore, that Lolly would choose to discover herself in a rural setting. But Garrity points out that because of a fusion of her love of the countryside and her communist political views, Townsend Warner did not feel that rural dwellers had a unique right to own land just because of their birthright, but that land should be 'shared' between those willing to work it. This is very different to the belief systems expressed by Mary Butts, who we will come on to later.

As with all of our Nature Mystics, the evidence for the love of nature, whether conscious or unconscious, comes out in their writing. For Townsend Warner (like both Webb and Keats) this love of nature becomes translated into a beauty that is evident in her arresting descriptions. It is nature that calls Lolly to witch-craft, with a description that includes the familiar pagan trope of the Wild Hunt, as the trees chant the Witches' Rune:

It was so warm in the woods that she forgot she sat there for shelter. But though the wind blew lightly, it blew from the east... The bright, cold fields were dimmed and warm to walk in now. Like embers the wet beech-leaves smouldered in the woods.

All one day the wind had risen, and late in the evening it called her out. She went up to the top of Cubbey Ridge, past the ruined windmill that clattered with its torn sails. When she had come to the top of the ridge she stopped, with difficulty holding herself upright. She felt the wind swoop down close to the earth. The moon was out hunting overhead, her pack of black and white hounds ranged over the sky. Moon and wind and clouds hunted an invisible quarry. The wind routed through the woods. Laura from the hill-top heard the various surrounding woods cry out with different voices. The spent gusts left the beech-hangers throbbing like sea caverns through which the wave had passed, the fir-plantation seemed to chant some never ending rune.

These are the elements that call the Modern Pagan to literature like this, and these descriptions seep their way into our traditions today, forming part of the poetry of ritual and prayer.

D.H. Lawrence (1885 – 1930)

David Herbert Lawrence was one of the most controversial writers in this series, both in his own time and ours. Readers and critics are unable to be lukewarm about Lawrence, but he is a 'Marmite man': some love his work and hail him as a misunderstood genius, while others find him a deeply offensive misogynist. Lawrence is most well known for his controversial novels, including *Lady Chatterley's Lover, The Rainbow, Sons and Lovers,* and *Women in Love,* but some of his most interesting work is less well known. Lawrence was a prolific and accomplished poet, he wrote some very intriguing short stories and also painted. Like his books, his paintings caused offence and were banned from being exhibited in the UK: they show a raw sexuality, and a confrontational aspect that was not acceptable during his lifetime. In terms of Nature Mysticism, Lawrence is probably the closest we will get to Mary Webb in this series. Like her, Lawrence too is often referred to as a Nature Mystic, as this is where he found his inspiration – he loved nothing more than to sit beneath a tree to write. Unlike Webb, he had a more nomadic lifestyle that took him around the world, largely due to the controversy he attracted in England.

Lawrence's Life: Putting His Work in Context

What value do we put on a human life? Most lives are rich in detail to the person living it, but are often distilled down into a few short sentences by those observing, skimming off only the most noticeable features. Lawrence's biography twists and turns, and yet for him too there were certain key details which came to define him as a man, and as an artist. For a reader of the autobiographical *Sons and Lovers,* the details of Lawrence's early beginnings will be familiar. Born in 1885 in Eastwood, Nottinghamshire, Lawrence was the fourth son of a barely literate miner, Arthur Lawrence, and a former pupil teacher, Lydia. While Lydia was educated, financial difficulties in her family had meant she was sent to work in a lace factory, and therefore never reached her academic potential. The young Lawrence won a scholarship to high school, and on leaving school in 1901 went on to become a junior clerk in a factory; however, a severe bout of pneumonia brought a halt to this career early on. His convalescence led to him spending a lot of time on the nearby Hagg's Farm, where he formed a relationship with Jessie Chambers, with whom he shared a mutual love of books. After fully recovering, Lawrence became a pupil teacher, and ultimately earned a qualification from the University of Nottingham. It was at this time that Lawrence began to write poems and short stories.

In 1908, as a newly qualified teacher, Lawrence left Nottingham for London, where he taught in a school in Croydon and continued to write. Jessie Chambers sent one of Lawrence's short stories to Ford Madox Ford at *The English Review*, and his work came to the attention of publishers. His first novel, *The White Peacock*, was commissioned, but shortly before publication in 1910 Lawrence's mother died of cancer. Lawrence's relationship with his mother was formative, and her death impacted on him severely. He spent a year deep in mourning, which he later referred to as his 'sick year', and many of his poems explore this grief. For anyone who has experienced similar deep grief, these poems, such as 'The Ship of Death', are very evocative.

In 1912, two events radically changed Lawrence's life. Firstly, he had a second bout of pneumonia, which led him finally to give up teaching to write full time, and he also met and fell in love with Frieda Weekley, the German wife of his languages professor in Nottingham. Frieda and Lawrence 'eloped' together, although it was to be several years before she could obtain a divorce and they could marry. It was this event that sparked the first of Lawrence's nomadic journeys around the world. From Germany,

Lawrence and Frieda walked across the Alps into Italy, while Lawrence continued to write, publishing *Sons and Lovers* in 1913, and starting work on *The Rainbow* and *Women in Love*, which he completed while living in Zennor, Cornwall, in 1916-17. While at Zennor, Lawrence also had a romantic affair with a local farmer, William Henry Hocking, although there are conflicting reports as to the sexual nature of this affair. This was not the first or last time Lawrence would find love in a same-sex relationship, and yet he remained with Frieda for the rest of his life. In 1914, shortly before the outbreak of World War One, Frieda obtained her divorce from her first husband, and she and Lawrence married.

Lawrence was now to experience the first overt disapproval from the establishment, which continued to dog him for the rest of his life. Marriage to a German wife and his own contempt for militarism meant suspicion was cast on Lawrence, and he was compelled to leave Cornwall following (unfounded) allegations of his signalling to German ships moored offshore: it was deemed too risky to have someone with questionable loyalty so close to the coastline. The couple also faced financial problems – *The Rainbow* was suppressed due to an allegation of obscenity, and lack of money and constant moving meant they were very poor. Following the war years, Lawrence and Frieda embarked on voluntary exile, and never returned to England for any great length of time. Their travelling took them to Australia, Italy, Sri Lanka, America, the South of France and Mexico. In these years, Lawrence continued to write and published eight novels, as well as numerous collections of plays, short stories, poems, travel writing, and essays. He also painted, although a gallery in London exhibiting his paintings was raided by the police, and following further charges of obscenity his artwork was never again exhibited in England in his lifetime.

In 1930, Lawrence died in France at the age of forty five, due to complications from tuberculosis; however, his story does not quite end there. Due to its controversial material, Lawrence's most infamous book was never published in full in his lifetime. A heavily censored version of *Lady Chatterley's Lover* was published in New York in 1928, but in 1960 Penguin chose to publish it in full. Penguin was then prosecuted under the newly established Obscene Publications Act of 1959, which made it possible for publishers to escape conviction if they could show an allegedly obscene work was of literary merit. The apparent problem with *Lady Chatterley* was not just the inter-class issue of a lady having a sexual affair with her game keeper, but the frequent use of explicit language. The jurors who returned a verdict of 'not guilty' against Penguin enabled the public to read the book in full for the first time, in 1961.

However, the controversy surrounding Lawrence was to continue for many years, as critics are divided on the topic of Lawrence's sexual politics. Some deem him to be questionable in his portrayal of women, as well as his views on the role of women (and men) in society, and this has been damaging to his reputation as a writer. Doris Lessing went so far as to refer to him as 'a misogynist and a scumbag' in her introduction to *The Fox*, whilst also acknowledging a deep love of his work: 'Pick up a Lawrence tale,' she writes, 'and the old magic begins working.' His writing is still rich and varied, and whatever the view of his politics, his work is well worth exploration.

Lawrence and Spirituality

Many of Lawrence's biographers note his close affinity with nature. As a child his parents (and in particular his father) encouraged him to learn the names of the plants and flowers he saw around him, and both parents exhibited a strong love of the natural world. Despite the industrial development around the mining village of Eastwood, it was still quintessentially a rural village at that time, and the surrounding countryside gave ample opportunity to indulge in this love. To colliers like his father, working in what would have been dark and depressing surroundings, the walk to the pits through the beautiful countryside provided a chance to find happiness in the beauty of their natural surroundings. Those who knew Lawrence personally (including his sister and Jessie Chambers) comment frequently on his highly-tuned sensory awareness of the natural world. Lady Cynthia Asquith commented that it was impossible to spend time in the outdoors with Lawrence without being aware of 'the astonishing acuteness of his senses, and realizing that he belonged to an intenser existence'. But this vision was also something he was able to share with those around him, through his written work and through conversation. Even those who disliked him (such as the Scottish composer Cecil Gray, who was his neighbour in Zennor) were able to recognise this facility. Gray described Lawrence as 'a faun, a child of Pan'. But there is a marked difference between loving the natural world, and building a spiritual life based on this love. One academic study[4] has drawn parallels between Lawrence's views of nature and oriental traditions and philosophies. This study notes that Lawrence had a particular affinity to trees, and often wrote while sitting beneath particular trees that he was drawn to. Frieda is quoted as saying that 'it was as if the tree itself helped him to write his book, and poured its sap into it'. In this way, *Lady Chatterley* was written in a wood of umbrella pines near Florence, and *The Fantasia of the Unconscious* was written in the Black Forest in Germany. Lawrence himself wrote:

> I lose myself among the trees. I am so glad to be with them in their silent, intent passion, and their great lust. They feel my soul.

This feeling of a soul connection to the trees is likened by the author of the study, to the Buddhist awakening, which leads to a sense of 'oneness with life and its environment', as well as Taoist philosophies, which connect the spiritual dimensions to nature, and it could be said of the Western esoteric world view also. However, his deep feeling of connection was not limited to trees or plants. Aldous Huxley noted that Lawrence did not just feel an affinity with nature, but was also able to 'get inside the skin of an animal and tell you in the most convincing detail how it felt and how... it thought'.

Lawrence may not have followed an organized path or belief system (which is not surprising since Western nature-based traditions really only took off as an organized spiritual path in the second half of the twentieth century). Lawrence certainly had a strong spiritual link with nature and took his inspiration for writing in a natural setting, just as Mary Webb did. Since Lawrence was well travelled, it is possible he may have come into contact with such philosophies, although his instinctive spiritual connection to nature seems to have developed long before his exile. It was this strong sense of spiritual connection to all aspects of nature, which then informed his writing in works such as *The Fox*.

Lawrence's Written Work

Whilst most people are familiar with Lawrence's major novels, there are two lesser known pieces that I will focus on in this chapter. The first is Lawrence's novella, *The Fox*, and the second is his poem 'The Ship of Death'.

The Fox was first published in 1923. Doris Lessing, in her introduction to *The Fox*, describes the novella as 'quintessential Lawrence, on the cusp as it were, of light and dark', and the story is certainly very haunting. The book concerns the story of two women, March and Banford, living alone on a farm at the end of the First World War, just as soldiers are beginning to return from the Western Front, broken and in pieces. At this time, so many men had simply not returned, it was common for women to be living together, and Lawrence does not reveal whether or not theirs was a sexual relationship, only that they share a deep love. Neither of the women takes naturally to farming, they are failing in their drive for independence, nor are they able to cope with the realities of farm life. When their cow becomes pregnant, the women who are 'afraid of the coming event, sold her in a panic'. They also find it difficult to cope with the 'strange illnesses' their other livestock develop. When a fox steps into their lives and begins to steal their chickens, they decide he must be shot, but he is too clever for them, and continues to evade the gun. March, the stronger of the two women, develops a strange affinity for the animal, becoming obsessed and coming under its 'spell':

> She took her gun again and went to look for the fox. For he had lifted his eyes upon her, and his knowing look seemed to have entered her brain. She did not so much think of him: she was possessed by him. She saw his dark, shrewd, unabashed eye looking into her, knowing her. She felt him invisibly master her spirit. She knew the way he lowered his chin as he looked up, she knew his muzzle, the golden brown, and the greyish white. And again she saw him glance over his shoulder at her, half inviting, half contemptuous and cunning. So she went, with her great startled eyes glowing, her gun under her arm, along the wood edge. Meanwhile the night fell, and a great moon rose above the pine trees.

March starts to dream about the fox, and the fox takes on qualities beyond its animal status; it represents the forbidden, the sensual, the animal nature that is hidden inside, and also masculinity. Into the space created by the fox, there comes a young man, a soldier newly returned from France, and he throws the world of the two women into complete disarray. The youth develops a strong and magnetic relationship with March, which leaves Banford in fear of exclusion, particularly when he announces that he and March will marry in a very short time.

The seemingly comfortable world the two women have created for themselves will never be the same again. According to Lessing, *The Fox* is 'quintessentially Lawrence'. She describes his writing as 'spellbinding', and that 'he knocks you over the head with the power of his identification with all that he sees'. It is Lawrence's deep connection to nature that is so compelling in *The Fox*, as it is not just the natural world that Lawrence identifies with, but also the animal nature contained within. The fox is not the only interloper and a thief, but the young man also. While March had previously worn men's breeches and was androgynous, she now starts to wear more feminine dresses and displays a vulnerability in femininity that wasn't clear before. A power struggle develops between the excluded Banford and the young soldier and they battle for March's affections, 'a subtle and profound battle of wills is taking place in the invisible,' writes Lawrence, and it can only be resolved in death.

While Lawrence's novella is haunting and evocative, his poetry is also intriguing. 'The Ship of Death' is a poem that is very close to my own heart[5]. It is an excellent example of Lawrence's exploration of the process of death and grieving following the loss of his mother. If it were to feature in a tarot deck, this would be a clear contender for the idea of the Death Card being interpreted as 'death and rebirth', and not a complete ending. But it is also the Six of Swords, a journey across water or liminal spaces, leading to a rebirth and an initiation of sorts. It begins with the lines:

Now it is autumn and the falling fruit
And the long journey towards oblivion
The apples falling like great drops of dew
To bruise themselves an exit from themselves
And it is time to go, to bid farewell
To one's own self, and find an exit
From the fallen self.

Lawrence encourages the reader to build their ship of death that will carry them to 'the deep and lovely quiet / of a strong heart at peace' and 'die the long and painful death / that lies between the old safe and the new'. For anyone with a strong sense of a deep inner life or spiritual path, the concept of 'death of the old self and the rebirth of the new' will not be an unfamiliar one. The poem speaks of transformation, of stepping over liminal gateways, and is evocative of the process of initiation where the old self is released in order to be transformed. As the darkness of oblivion descends, Lawrence speaks of hope:

> And yet out of eternity a thread
> Separates itself on the blackness
> A horizontal thread
> That fumes a little with pallor upon the dark

The dark flood subsides, and the body emerges 'like a worn sea-shell / emerges strange and lovely', and the ship of death returns home allowing the 'frail soul' to step once more 'into the house again / filling the heart with peace'. The poem concludes with the lines:

> Oh build your ship of death, oh build it!
> For you will need it
> For the voyage of oblivion awaits you

For those grieving the death of a most beloved one (just like Lawrence) the poem not only speaks of the inevitable journey into the darkness that we all must face in our own mortality, but also, that the process of grief inevitably changes a person irrevocably. Life will never be the same again following a significant loss, and yet one must rebuild a life that is worthy of the memory of a loved one.

Elizabeth von Arnim (1866 – 1941)

Like most of the women writers in this series, Elizabeth von Arnim is largely unknown to contemporary readers. This is in vibrant contrast to the very successful writing career she enjoyed during her own lifetime. However, more recently her name has popped up in several places, leading to a mini-resurgence. A copy of her book *Elizabeth and Her German Garden* made a fleeting appearance in Downton Abbey, and her publishers then deftly issued *The Enchanted April* in a beautiful edition covered in Liberty fabric, and listeners to Open Book (on BBC Radio 4) voted her one of their favourite forgotten writers.

Like several of our other Nature Mystics, von Arnim too had a life story almost more fantastical than the plots of her novels. I say *almost* because von Arnim frequently used her own life as the (loose) blueprint for her novels. For instance, her first novel, *Elizabeth and Her German Garden*, published in 1898, was based on her own marriage and life in Germany. She was also writing on the cusp of the nineteenth and twentieth centuries, just as the curtains of Victorian England were parting to make way for a new century, and a new zeitgeist.

Publishing twenty one novels over the course of her lifetime, von Arnim's work is difficult for academics to classify, since the novels follow a range of topics and styles; however, the thing that unites them is von Arnim's love of nature, which suffuses all the narratives with the beauty of the natural world. As Miranda Kiek wrote, 'Where Woolf said every woman needed a room of her own, von Arnim would have said every woman needed a garden.'[6] Thus this love of nature, and her writing on that love of nature, brings von Arnim to our table with the other Nature Mystics.

Von Arnim's Life: Putting Her Work in Context

Von Arnim was a deeply involved member of the literati of the early twentieth century, but despite this there is a scarcity of information available about her. (If anyone has a spare year or two, there is definitely a gap in the market for a biographical study of her). Born in Kirribilli Point, Australia, as Mary Annette Beauchamp in 1866, von Arnim was the daughter of a merchant. The family owned a holiday home at Kirribilli Point, but returned to England when von Arnim was three, where she spent the rest of her happy childhood. As the youngest of four brothers, a sister and an adopted cousin, she is reported to have been quite solitary and 'bookish'. Superficially, this family life might seem fairly mundane, but her cousin was Kathleen Beauchamp, who later married John Middleton Murray and wrote novels and short stories under the nom de plume of Katherine Mansfield.

Whilst on a tour of Italy with her father, Elizabeth met Prussian aristocrat Count Henning August von Arnim-Schlagenthin, and they were married in 1891. Their married life began in Berlin, then moved to the family estate at Nassenheide in the Pomeranian countryside. Despite its rural setting, von Arnim still moved in literary circles: among her children's tutors were E.M. Forster and Hugh Walpole. Although they had four daughters and a son, the marriage was not a particularly happy one, and it was the troubles in her marriage that spurred von Arnim into writing. Her husband (who she referred to as the 'Man of Wrath' in her novels) had financial problems, and was even sent to prison for fraud. Forced to generate an income, she launched her writing career, and her first novel was published in 1898. *Elizabeth and Her German Garden* was a huge success, being reprinted twenty times within the first year of its publication. To retain some anonymity (presumably to protect her husband and his family, as the satirical novel poked fun at them), von Arnim published her first few books under the name of 'the author of

Elizabeth's German Garden', or simply 'by Elizabeth'. But in 1908 she left the 'Man of Wrath' and returned to England; in 1910, he died. From 1910 to 1913, von Arnim became one of H.G. Wells' lovers, making her unpopular with Rebecca West (another of Wells' mistresses). In 1916, von Arnim married John Russell, the second Earl Russell and older brother of Bertrand; sadly, again the marriage was unhappy and the couple separated in 1919, although they never divorced. Von Arnim continued to have various relationships, but never again remarried.

In 1939, von Arnim travelled to the United States where she died in 1941 from influenza, at the age of seventy four. She was cremated, and her ashes were mingled with those of her brother in a churchyard in Tyler's Green, Buckinghamshire.

Von Arnim and Spirituality

For a series about Nature Mystics, unfortunately this section of the chapter is going to be the shortest of all the Nature Mystics. None of the biographical material I have read thus far mentions anything about von Arnim's spiritual life. There is clearly a large gap in the research about her, as most biographical studies concentrate on her relationships and her dramatic life path, rather than her spiritual beliefs. One thing that is certain is her deep connection with nature, which is how she finds her way into this series, and her ability to find peace when in nature, which is borne out in most of her work. Most studies take this love of nature at face value, and do not question whether this spills into, or correlates with, a belief system. Instead of trying to extrapolate some sense of von Arnim's spiritual life, this article will move on to the ways in which nature permeates her written work, while acknowledging there is a gap in the academic record that needs to be filled. As we have seen with previous Nature Mystics, it is a short hop from a life drenched with a love of nature, to embracing it in its most spiritual aspects.

Von Arnim's Written Work

Following the publication of her first novel, *Elizabeth and Her German Garden*, in 1898, von Arnim went on to publish twenty more books. The first few capitalized on the popularity of her first, but she was also to go on and diversify her novels considerably. The two novels I have chosen to concentrate on are *Vera* (1921) and *The Enchanted April* (1922).

Vera is a deeply disturbing thriller, very much in the vein of Daphne du Maurier's 1938 novel *Rebecca* (although of course, as *Vera* came first it actually anticipates *Rebecca*). Said by Nicola Beauman to be 'a ferocious and at times macabre indictment' of Elizabeth's second husband, John Russell, if this were true and if the novel is anything to go by, it is no surprise that their marriage failed so quickly. But the book is interesting for this study in two ways: not only are the details of the natural world very vivid, but it is also a very precise and insightful study of human nature. Like Keats, von Arnim is a Human Nature Mystic. Like the young wife in *Rebecca*, the protagonist is a naïve young woman, Lucy Entwhistle, who, left alone and afraid following the death of her father, is comforted by a recently widowed Everard Wemyss, whom she meets suddenly one day while in the garden of their home in Cornwall. Wemyss is a tower of strength in the immediate aftermath of her loss, but there is always an uncomfortable edge:

It was Wemyss who had done all the thinking for her, and in the spare moments between his visits to the undertaker about the arrangements, and to the doctor about the certificate, and to the vicar about the burial, and telegraphed to her only existing relative, an aunt, had sent the obituary notice to The Times, and had even reminded her that she had on a blue frock and asked if she hadn't better put on a black one; and now this last instance of his thoughtfulness overwhelmed her.

Of course, the idea of a man doing 'all the thinking' or telling a woman what to wear has sinister overtones to our contemporary understanding of control and abuse. What begins as 'thoughtfulness' soon becomes oppression as Lucy then finds herself swept into a hasty marriage. Wemyss describes himself and Lucy as 'two scared, unhappy children, clinging to each other alone in the dark', and takes Lucy to live at his family home, The Willows, where he begins to treat her like a naughty child. It is here that life starts to unravel, as Lucy begins to be haunted (although not literally) by the traces of his first wife Vera, who died under mysterious circumstances. Lucy begins to regret her hasty marriage as she learns that The Willows is run by Everard's increasingly domineering household routines, and finds herself progressively more and more isolated from her only living relative, Aunt Dot, and subject to Everard's control. The book itself, like *Rebecca*, is well paced and gripping as the story builds to its conclusion, and it leaves you with a feeling of unease long after you have finished reading. This is partly because the reader is never really sure if Everard was responsible for the death of his first wife, or what his intentions really are with regards to Lucy.

But not all of von Arnim's works are so uncomfortable to read. *The Enchanted April* is both captivating and as reassuring as a warm bath. The story tells of two ladies, Mrs Lotty Wilkins and Mrs Rose Arbuthnot, who both decide to flee their unhappy Hampstead lives to spend a month in an Italian castle, San Salvatore. What begins as a way of escaping the drudgery of their lives in London becomes a transformative and magical experience. Both Rose and Lotty are troubled by their marriages. Rose (a passionately godly woman) is married to Frederick Arbuthnot, the writer of salacious popular biographies of which she deeply disapproves, whilst Lotty's husband Mellersh Wilkins is a dull solicitor who long ago sacrificed his heart to business.

The two women themselves are also opposites. Rose is very steady:

Steadfast as the points of the compass to Mrs. Arbuthnot were the great four facts of life: God, Husband, Home, Duty. She had gone to sleep on these facts years ago, after a period of much misery, her head resting on them as on a pillow; and she had a great dread of being awakened out of so simple and untroublesome a condition.

Lotty, however, is very unsteady, and (very gently) knocks those around her off balance too. When they first meet, having both found the advert in The Times for 'those who appreciate wisteria and sunshine', von Arnim writes that Rose:

> ...sat and looked uneasily at Mrs. Wilkins, feeling more and more the urgent need to getting her classified. If she could only classify Mrs. Wilkins, get her safely under her proper heading, she felt that she herself would regain her balance, which did seem very strangely to be slipping all to one side.

Lotty then, not only knocks Rose off-balance, but she is also unlike anyone Rose has met before; her slightly scatty exterior belies a wealth of talents underneath. Lotty also has a knack of presciently anticipating events – she is clear that the women need to be at San Salvatore so it can 'work its magic' on them long before Rose is convinced:

> 'It's so funny,' said Mrs. Wilkins, just as if she had not heard her, 'But I see us both—you and me—this April in the mediaeval castle.'
> Mrs. Arbuthnot relapsed into uneasiness. 'Do you?' she said, making an effort to stay balanced under the visionary gaze of the shining grey eyes. 'Do you?'
> 'Don't you ever see things in a kind of flash before they happen?' asked Mrs. Wilkins.
> 'Never,' said Mrs. Arbuthnot.

There is something distinctly supernatural about Lotty's abilities, and her 'visionary gaze' enables her to very gently steer people towards the outcome that will be best for them, whilst maintaining an exterior impression of mundane scattiness.

In order to be able to afford the rent, they advertise to find two other women to join them; but, as they only receive two replies, they don't have much choice. Lady Caroline Dester (known to her friends as Scrap) is a beautiful society girl emotionally exhausted by all the attention she gets and looking for respite and retreat; Mrs Fisher is a cantankerous older lady who calmly assumes the complete organisation of the household. But the magic that awaits them at San Salvatore soon transforms all four women. As they spend time in the beautiful grounds around the castle, their own stories start to unravel, and we see characters who have a vulnerable underbellies. Scrap, like many young women of this time, is depressed having lost the 'only man she could have ever loved' in the First World War, and Mrs Fisher starts to face how lonely she really is. Lotty was adamant that they were the right people for San Salvatore, despite their questionable surface appearance, and time spent in the beautiful gardens seems to bear this out.

And it is in von Arnim's descriptions of the gardens around San Salvatore that the magic really starts to unfold and profoundly affect the women (and men) who come there. From the moment they arrive at the place in the dark, the castle and its grounds seem to exist outside of the mundane world. Even in the darkness, there is an enchanting quality to the nature that soaks the castle grounds. Although they cannot see them, the women know the garden is full of flowers:

They crossed a little bridge, over what was apparently a ravine, and then came a flat bit with long grass at the sides and more flowers. They felt the grass flicking wet against their stockings, and the invisible flowers were everywhere. Then up again through trees, along a zigzag path with the smell all the way of the flowers they could not see. The warm rain was bringing out all the sweetness. Higher and higher they went in this sweet darkness, and the red light on the jetty dropped farther and farther below them.

When they awake the next morning, Lottie knows she will see the most beautiful scenery, and takes her time in going to the window, enjoying the sense of sweet anticipation. But it is the description of what she sees when she does look that take von Arnim's work over the edge from simple 'nature loving' to Nature Mysticism; that sense of bliss and divine communion that is gained from time spent absorbed in the natural world. She describes the first view from San Salvatore thus, and transports us to the coast of Italy:

All the radiance of April in Italy lay gathered together at her feet. The sun poured in on her. The sea lay asleep in it, hardly stirring. Across the bay the lovely mountains, exquisitely different in colour, were asleep too in the light; and underneath her window, at the bottom of the flower-starred grass slope from which the wall of the castle rose up, was a great cypress, cutting through the delicate blues and violets and rose-colours of the mountains and the sea like a great black sword.

She stared. Such beauty; and she there to see it. Such beauty; and she alive to feel it. Her face was bathed in light. Lovely scents came up to the window and caressed her. A tiny breeze gently lifted her hair. Far out in the bay a cluster of almost motionless fishing boats hovered like a flock of white birds on the tranquil sea. How beautiful, how beautiful. Not to have died before this . . . to have been allowed to see, breathe, feel this. . . . She stared, her lips parted. Happy? Poor, ordinary, everyday word. But what could one say, how could one describe it? It was as though she could hardly stay inside herself, it was as though she were too small to hold so much of joy, it was as though she were washed through with light. And how astonishing to feel this sheer bliss, for here she was, not doing and not going to do a single unselfish thing, not going to do a thing she didn't want to do.

The beauty of the natural world surpasses all expectations, and captures the women in a cloak of pure life. They are transported beyond the everyday to something more magical. For the first time, all the women are able to slough off their duty-given identities. At San Salvatore they can spend their days in simply pleasing themselves, in enjoying the freedom of the bountiful gardens and the shoreline, and the magic of the place (and of nature) starts to transform them at an almost molecular level. As they surrender to the 'irresistible influence of the heavenly atmosphere of San Salvatore' they start to unfurl and bloom like rose buds. Being in that space changes their perceptions of their lives back at home, and they are freed from fretting about the problems of the mundane world, being are absorbed in something sacred, mystical and transformative; all they can do is surrender to the ineffable quality of the place.

She tried to visualize Mellersh, she tried to see him having breakfast and thinking bitter things about her; and lo, Mellersh himself began to shimmer, became rose-colour, became delicate violet, became an enchanting blue, became formless, became iridescent. Actually Mellersh, after quivering a minute, was lost in light.

'Well,' thought Mrs. Wilkins, staring, as it were, after him. How extraordinary not to be able to visualize Mellersh; and she who used to know every feature, every expression of his by heart. She simply could not see him as he was. She could only see him resolved into beauty, melted into harmony with everything else. The familiar words of the General Thanksgiving came quite naturally into her mind, and she found herself blessing God for her creation, preservation, and all the blessings of this life, but above all for His inestimable Love; out loud; in a burst of acknowledgment.

Lady Caroline finds the peace she desperately needed, and begins to emerge from her deep depression and dissatisfaction with life; Mrs Fisher starts to defrost and become more approachable, while Rose and Lotty both begin to re-connect with what was missing in their lives. When they arrive, even Mellersh Wilkins and Frederick Arbuthnot start to release their tight grip on a world that has lost all magic to them. They begin to find, at San Salvatore, that which they didn't even know they were missing.

The book is delightful, and bewitching, and well worth reading. While biographies of von Arnim may lack detail of her true relationship to the natural world, the sense of sacred connection that suffuses her writing is clear, and unavoidable. The biographical 'truth' of von Arnim's spiritual connection to the natural world may be missing in the academic record, but it is laid out beautifully in her writing.

William Butler Yeats (1865 – 1939)

To any student of English or Irish literature, William Butler Yeats will be a very well-known figure. One of the foremost figures of early twentieth century literature, his poetry and plays are frequently found on the academic syllabus. However, not every reader might be aware that he was also one of the foremost figures in esotericism at the time, particularly in the Western Ceremonial tradition. Yeats was at the heart of several groups that would be familiar to any student of the occult, yet the wide range of his activities might be surprising. Yeats participated in the Theosophical Society with Madame Blavatsky, had an interest in Spiritualism, experimented widely with automatic writing and was at the very heart of the Hermetic Order of the Golden Dawn, and its later re-named incarnation, Stella Matutina. Yeats' active occult life also translated into his written work, which is rich in Irish folklore, and also in occult symbols – the tarot, the concept of masks, Kabbalah, and Mysticism.

In later years he downplayed his involvement in esoterica for the sake of his literary reputation. However, recent scholars suggest that his occult interests never really left him. Instead, he cultivated a 'mask' that was worn in public life that shielded his spiritual life from prying eyes. If this study did not examine Yeats as a key influence on Modern Paganism, it would be missing a crucial figure.

Yeats' Life: Putting His Work in Context
William Butler Yeats was born in Dublin in 1865. His father, John Butler Yeats, originally trained to be a lawyer, but abandoned his studies in favour of becoming an artist, and later became well known for his portraits. His mother was the daughter of a wealthy merchant family from Sligo. Yeats was educated both in London and Dublin, but summers were spent at the family's

home in County Sligo. This was to be a landscape Yeats was to love for the rest of his life. In 1867 the family moved to London to further John's career as an artist, and for some time William and his siblings were educated at home by their parents; his mother first introduced the young William to Irish folk tales and legends, while his father taught them chemistry and geography, and took them on expeditions to the nearby countryside. In 1877 Yeats went to the Godolphin school, but was not considered to be a particularly good student, due to his 'poor spelling'. In 1880, the family returned to Dublin because of financial pressures, but Yeats was more interested in spending time at his father's studio than at school, where he met an array of artistic people. Significantly, all four children were to become artistic in their endeavours; his brother Jack became a painter, while his two sisters, Elizabeth and Susan Mary, became involved in The Arts and Crafts Movement.

At the age of seventeen, Yeats began to write poetry, at first influenced by Shelley, and later by William Blake. Blake planted a seed for Yeats' later interest in the esoteric life, but the signs were there early enough: Yeats' first poem was written about a magician, and his first play concerned a woman in a rural community who was accused of paganism. In 1885, at the age of twenty, Yeats was involved in the formation of the Dublin Hermetic Order and became its chairman. He also attended meetings of the Dublin Theosophical Society, and attended his first séance. This interest in the occult was to remain with Yeats for the rest of his life.

In 1887, the family returned to London and Yeats' first volume of poetry was published that same year. Once back in London, Yeats met Madame Blavatsky, and joined the Theosophical Society in 1888. Soon after, Yeats met Maude Gonne, a relationship that was to have a lasting effect on him. Maude Gonne became Yeats' muse, as well as the woman with whom he was to have a very complex relationship for the next twenty years or so. Maud Gonne joined Yeats in being initiated into the Hermetic Order of the Golden Dawn in 1890.

Over the next few years, as the nineteenth century turned into the twentieth, Yeats' literary career took off, and he completed several lecture tours around America. He was a very successful playwright and poet, and was involved in various influential projects, such as the Abbey Theatre in Dublin and the Cuala Press, which he established with his sisters, that published his work alongside that of Ezra Pound and Elizabeth Bowen. His esoteric life also flourished and this became the fuel that kept his literary fires still burning.

Sadly, his private life was not quite as successful. His relationship with Maud Gonne swung from platonic, to a state of 'it's complicated', which was made more thorny by Maud's rejection of Yeats' three proposals of marriage, and her subsequent marriage to the Irish Nationalist John McBride in 1903. To Yeats' added horror, Maude also converted to Catholicism, which took her ever further out of his reach and into the influence of the priests. She was to separate from her husband in 1904, and she and Yeats eventually consummated their relationship four years later. However, the relationship did not develop in the way Yeats had hoped it would and they separated soon after. Maude Gonne was adamant that she could not be Yeats' muse as well as his lover. She believed it was his unrequited love for her that spurred him on to writing his best poetry. On rejecting his proposal, she is alleged to have told Yeats that one day the world would thank her for ensuring that he continued to write to his best ability. In truth, by the end, Gonne and Yeats were not suited to each other – she wanted a relationship that supported her Catholicism and Irish Nationalism, while Yeats wanted a magical partner. Sadly, although she found what she wanted on paper, Gonne's marriage to John McBride also ended tragically. Although they separated soon into the marriage in 1904, they never divorced. McBride was later executed in 1916, along with John Connelly and the other leaders of The Easter Uprising.

However, the Yeats-Gonne relationship did not quite end there and continued to become further complex. By the time he reached his early fifties, Yeats decided he wanted a wife to help him produce an heir. He also wanted someone to work with him on his esoteric projects involving channelling, automatic writing (and allegedly sex magic). At this point, Yeats became convinced that it was not Maud Gonne, but her daughter Iseult that he was meant to be with. Iseult had lived quite a sad life, having been conceived as an attempt to re-incarnate her late brother. Furthermore, she was presented as Maud's 'niece' for the first few years of her life. Although Iseult had proposed to Yeats when she was fifteen, at the age of twenty one she had other ideas. When Iseult also rejected him, Yeats went on to marry George Hyde Lees, with whom he had two children and also a successful magical partnership. George experimented with channelling and automatic writing with Yeats, and although he was not entirely faithful to her, they remained married until his death.

In his later life, Yeats continued to achieve success with his writing. He moved in literary circles all his life, interacting with many other movers and shakers of nineteenth and twentieth century arts, from Oscar Wilde to Ezra Pound. To this end, Yeats spanned the gap between nineteenth and twentieth century literature. He was awarded an honorary degree from Trinity College, Dublin, in 1922, and also the Nobel Prize in Literature in 1923. He continued to write right up until his death in 1939 at the age of seventy three. He died in France and was buried there, but was later re-interred in County Sligo.

Yeats and Spirituality

Later in life, when Yeats was working closely with the young Ezra Pound and was also in contact with T.S. Eliot, he is alleged to have given up his esoteric practices. Pound (who acted as

Yeats' secretary for some time) and Eliot both felt Yeats' interest in the occult was rather silly, and Yeats knew he needed to be taken seriously or his literary reputation would suffer. He had faced some opposition from the Church, which believed him to be heretical in his practices. More recent scholarship, however, has suggested that this was simply a divide between Yeats' public and private lives to ensure that he was taken seriously in scholarly circles. Although in public he did not appear to be 'dabbling in the occult', his private practices continued as they had before. Many biographies therefore discuss Yeats' esoteric practices as something he did in younger life, before settling down to more serious scholarly pursuits as he got older.

In truth, Yeats' spiritual life was central to his work as a poet all of his life. In a letter to John O'Leary in 1892, Yeats wrote, 'The mystical life is the centre of all that I do and all that I think and all that I write.' According to Susan Johnston Graf, 'Yeats placed the poet at the meeting point between Heaven and Earth, defining him as one possessed by a divinity, an oracle through whom a daimon might find a voice.'[7] The poet, then, was synonymous with the magus for Yeats. But it is also Yeats' beliefs regarding the concept of this 'daimon' that is key to unlocking some of Yeats' spiritual beliefs. When he began the work of the second degree in the Golden Dawn in 1893, Yeats took the motto 'Demon est Deus inversus', which over the years has been mistranslated and has therefore caused some confusion. While a more simplistic Christian-influenced translation might read 'the Devil is the opposite of God', Graf suggests an alternative translation is necessary. In its original Latin form, 'daemon' does not translate as devil (diabolus) but as a spirit, or genius, that would inspire a human to produce great work. Prior to the Enlightenment, genius was seen as an external force or being that a writer had as opposed to the post-enlightenment belief that genius was something an artist was. By this rationale, genius was something external that visited and was not inherent in a person, and it could present its gifts where it wished, and also take them away. In addition, in the Kabbalistic Tree of Life, which Yeats spent many years studying, the earthly realm is placed at the bottom of the tree, while the attainment of god is placed at the top, and thus the daimon in Yeats' motto is an expression of divinity that emanates down to mankind. Graf therefore writes that, "Demon est Deus Inversus' labelled Yeats as one who recognised that a genius descends to its chosen human and invests him with power.'[8] The role of the human in this transaction is to cultivate the relationship, nurture it, and make good use of the visiting daimon or genius. Philip Pullman takes up this idea of the daimon being an external creature in *His Dark Materials*, in creating a world where each human is accompanied through life with their daemon, just as Lyra Silvertongue is accompanied by Pantalaimon.

Yeats' time in London brought him into contact with some of the most influential figures in the esoteric world at that time. For a time he worked with Madame Blavatsky at the Theosophical Society, until he questioned some of their beliefs and attracted the displeasure of the Theosophical leadership. He then met Samuel McGregor Mathers at the British Museum, where he was undertaking research. Mathers invited Yeats to join the Golden Dawn, and he remained as part of this group until 1923. During the thirty three years of his involvement, Yeats would have worked with Mathers, Woodman, Annie Horniman, Pamela Colman Smith and Arthur Waite (who developed the Rider-Waite tarot deck), Florence Farr, Israel Regardie (who wrote widely on Kabbalah), Arnold Bennett, Algernon Blackwood, Dion Fortune, Arthur Machen, Bram Stoker, Evelyn Underhill (who wrote widely on Christian Mysticism), Edith Nesbit and not forgetting, Aleister Crowley. Yeats' relationship with Crowley, however, was not one of friendly co-operation. In 1900, seeing problems within the leadership of the Golden Dawn, Yeats attempted a take-over, and in response Yeats' former mentor Mathers sent his newest adept, Crowley, to take over the temple. Yeats (and others) successfully barred the way to Crowley in what came to be known as 'The Battle of Blythe Road', but Yeats and Crowley were never to see eye to eye, and in consequence, they were to remain lifelong enemies.

Yeats' poetry makes frequent references to the occult and is rich in esoteric symbolism, particularly with regards to Kabbalah, Rosicrucianism, and the tarot, and because Yeats is still known as a symbolist poet, some of the deeper layers of meanings go under the radar for readers unfamiliar with esotericism. Yeats produced two works which were overt in his occult practices. The first was *Per Amica Silentia Lunae* which he wrote and published in 1918. Yeats intended *Per Amica* to be a treatise of his spiritual beliefs and took the title from a line from *The Aeneid*, in which the invading forces lie in wait within the walls of the city of Troy, concealed within the belly of the wooden horse, 'under the friendly silence of a still moon'. Coincidentally (or not) Mary Webb's husband, Henry Bertram Law Webb, had published a similar volume just three years before, entitled *The Silences of the Moon*, in which he put forward his beliefs in occultism and proposed that what was lacking in the modern age was a deep connection to nature. In *Per Amica*, Yeats recorded his spiritual history and beliefs and at the time he felt it was his key work. Writing at the age of fifty two, it demonstrated that Yeats' strong belief in the occult was still with him. A decade later, he had withdrawn from public activities, and had drawn a distinct line between public and private practice. The book was published originally with a depiction of a rose on the cover, which was evocative of the Golden Dawn's rose.

Despite the fact that Yeats' volume was addressed 'To My Dear 'Maurice'' (Iseult Gonne), his subsequent marriage to George was a successful one, and the couple carried out many experiments with automatic writing in their home. George was able to channel spirits and guides they referred to as 'Instructors'.

Whenever these spirits were ready to communicate with George they would signal this intent by filling the house with the smell of fresh mint leaves. Working closely with the Instructors, Yeats and George developed a complex system of characters and symbols relating to the 'gyre' (which appears in Yeats' poem 'The Second Coming'). While in oceanography the gyre is a complex system of spiralling currents, Yeats proposed the gyre as a spiral in time, which spanned two thousand years. The second of his overtly occult works was *A Vision* (1925), which Yeats believed surpassed *Per Amica* as his key work. *A Vision* contained more detail of the practices he carried out with George. While many thought the marriage between Yeats and George Hyde Lees would be unsuccessful due to the age difference, and the fact that Yeats was fifty two when they married, their partnership was fruitful and happy, and it enabled Yeats to continue writing right up until his death.

Yeats' Written Work

Yeats' written work tends to be characterized into three distinct periods. His earlier work explores the themes of his growing interest in the mystical, while the middle period (influenced by Pound and the Modernists) moves further away from these themes and becomes more technically proficient (although somehow lacking in passion). His later work, influenced by the work he and George were doing at home, returns to the mystical and the occult, and is closer to his vision in his earlier poems. Writing about Yeats' poetry is challenging; his use of language is so exquisitely precise that it is impossible to find 'better' ways to express Yeats' own thoughts and ideas.

'The Second Coming', written in 1920, is one of Yeats' most well-known poems, and contains some of the most memorable imagery of the twentieth century. If strength of poetry was to be measured by how many works it in turn influences, 'The Second Coming' could be one of the most significant poems of the twentieth century. It has been the inspiration behind many other creative works, such as Chinua Achebe's 1958 novel, *Things Fall Apart*, which took its title from a line in the poem, and also Joni Mitchel's song 'Slouching Towards Bethlehem (The Second Coming)' where she sets the poem to music. While some interpret the poem as Yeats' lament for the shortcomings of the Modernist age, it also expresses a vision of some of his more spiritual beliefs and still holds resonance for anyone who is politically or esoterically minded today. The poem begins with a description of the current state of society as the narrator sees it, and incorporates Yeats' complex ideas about the gyre:

Turning and turning in the widening gyre
The falcon cannot hear the falconer
Things fall apart; the centre cannot hold;
Mere anarchy is loosed upon the world,
The blood-dimmed tide is loosed, and everywhere
The ceremony of innocence is drowned.
The best lack all conviction, while the worst
Are full of passionate intensity.

Yeats describes the spiral formed gyre that is now becoming wider, having been turning for 'twenty centuries', but the centre of this gyre is unstable, and 'cannot hold'. Things will inevitably begin to fall apart. The falcon can no longer hear its handler, society starts to disintegrate, and a blood tide sweeps in across the land. Yeats describes a loss of innocence in the world, as the 'best lack conviction'. In other words, the most moral minded and greatest people are rendered inert and lack the conviction to make changes, while 'the worst' are full of passion, but lack mercy and empathy. The narrator then goes on to suggest that this state of confusion and anarchy cannot continue, 'Surely some revelation is at hand / Surely the Second Coming is at Hand'.

As these words are spoken, a vision appears of the 'Spiritus

Mundi' – the spirit of the world. Somewhere in the desert, a sphinx-like creature starts to move across the desert sands, with the body of a lion, and a man's head, 'and a gaze as pitiless as the sun'. The desert birds wheel around it, indignant at its grotesque appearance, before the darkness falls once more. But the 'twenty centuries of stony sleep' have taken their toll, and now 'what rough beast, its hour come at last / Slouches towards Bethlehem to be born'. It is interesting to note that although Yeats had moved away from organised religion in his quest for the occult, much of the imagery evoked in Yeats' vision of an apocalyptic world is still Abrahamic in essence (by which term I am referring to Christianity, Islam and Judaism). It is still the possibility of the 'second' coming of a messianic figure that will provide some relief, the birthplace evoked is Bethlehem (even if this location is symbolic as opposed to literal). Even the concept of a form of Armageddon is deeply rooted in Abrahamic symbolism. Although some of these archetypes appear across many world religions, and are not confined to the Abrahamic traditions, these are powerful symbols most commonly connected to them. While Yeats' symbolist imagery is intentionally grotesque and disturbing, and his system of gyres is quite complex, the feeling of discomfort evoked by the poem is haunting.

Not all of his poetry is this unsettling. 'The Lake Isle of Innisfree', published in his second volume of poems *The Rose* in 1893, evokes very different feelings than 'The Second Coming'. Already working with the Golden Dawn by this stage, the volume contains many poems that evoke the hermetic imagery of the order (the clue being in the name, 'The Rose', which was one of the order's most potent symbols). In 'The Lake Island of Innisfree' Yeats describes an island paradise he longs to return to, where he can exist in perfect simplicity with nature.

I will arise and go now, and go to Innisfree
And a small cabin build there, of clay and wattles made;

Nine bean-rows will I have there, a hive for the honeybee,
And live alone in the bee-loud glade.

For any who have fantasised about leaving the rat-race behind and escaping to a more simplistic existence, 'The Lake Isle of Innisfree' is a poignant symbol of a life lived closer to the land and without the complex trappings of society. But it is often used in funerals too, as a vivid description of a heavenly place that the lost loved one might have travelled to. Yeats writes that he shall find tranquillity at Innisfree, for 'peace comes dropping slow' from the leaves that hang above the glade where the 'cricket sings' and the evening is full of the gentle sounds of 'linnet's wings'. A vision of taking care of a garden, growing vegetables and tending beehives is one of peaceful simplicity and non-striving that would appeal to anyone wishing to live a mindful life. Yeats' wish to 'live alone' is not one of loneliness, but one of solitude, and peacefulness. As the last stanza reveals:

I will arise and go now, for always night and day
I hear lake water lapping with low sounds by the shore;
While I stand on the roadway, or on the pavements grey
I hear it in the deep heart's core

Yeats is imagining 'The Lake Isle of Innisfree' while standing on the grey pavements of the city (which would probably have been London). The vision is so clear to him, that he is able to transport himself away from the busy hustle of the city streets, and hear the gentle lapping of the lake water on the shore. This is so compelling that he hears the call of nature deep inside his heart in spite of his urban surroundings. Yeats may not have placed the sacred aspects of nature for nature's sake at the centre of his work in the way that some of our other Nature Mystics did, but nature was still the sound he heard in his heart and connected him to his soul. Innisfree is thought to be representative of Sligo, thus also demonstrating that his link to his sacred land in Ireland endured as long as his passion for the esoteric. Despite the long years of absence from Sligo, it still remained clear and strong in his imagination, and therefore his poetry.

Mary Butts (1890 – 1937)

Mary Butts is by far the most controversial subject of this series, perhaps even more so than Lawrence. Despite her being relatively unknown to the wider public, in more recent years more academic (and some esoteric attention) has been directed towards Butts. Her work has been undergoing somewhat of a critical and occult revival, which many believe is overdue after so many years of critical obscurity. Mary Butts is not someone to feel lukewarm about. To some she is an overlooked and underrated 'Sapphic Modernist'; to others she is a strong proponent of environmentalist views. On the flip side, Virginia Woolf described her as 'malignant' and the writer of indecent books (although Woolf was frequently dismissive of other female writers) and a visit from Butts left Woolf with a headache. Aleister Crowley described her as a 'large white red-haired maggot' (or words to that effect). On paper she *should* be a perfect example of an early twentieth century occult writer; a former student of Crowley's, she was credited as a co-author of his *Book Four*. Her novels explore themes that include a strong relationship with the land, the links between women, women's mysteries and the Great Goddess, as well as magic and mysticism. However, more recent scholars have pointed out that this is pitted against some very unsavoury political beliefs on Butts' part, that have been largely overlooked by her most ardent advocates. While it may be unfair to allow a writer's political beliefs to colour our assessment of their literary contribution, if Butts is to be given a balanced evaluation as a writer (and an occultist), it would be remiss to ignore the belief system that underscores her work.

Butts' Life: Putting Her Work in Context

The turn of the century was a time of great change and upheaval in the Western world. It was also a period of political change, and one of great opportunity. Mary Butts was born in 1890 into a wealthy family which lived at Salterns, an eighteenth century house overlooking Poole Harbour in Dorset. Salterns, and the Dorset landscape, were to become a major influence in Butts' development and beliefs. Wessex, and the house that she believed was her birthright, also became Butts' 'sacred landscape', against which every other landscape was measured. The house itself was filled with a number of original William Blake works, as Blake had been a family friend. These works had a significant impact on Butts, and included a painting of Hecate. When Butts' father died in 1904, her mother sold the Blake works, much to Mary's distress (these works eventually became housed at the Tate). Two years later she re-married, sent Mary to school in St Andrews in Scotland, and sold Salterns. Mary Butts was then, in effect, exiled from her beloved home and throughout her lifetime she believed that her mother had mismanaged her inheritance, which should have been protected at all costs. Butts became estranged from her mother and their relationship never recovered.

From 1909 onwards, Butts lived in London, first enrolling at Westfield College (part of the University of London) from which she was expelled in 1912. She went on to graduate from the London School of Economics two years later with a diploma (in the equivalent of modern day social work). She worked in London during the early part of the First World War, initially doing voluntary work for the Children's Care Committee in East London and later working with Conscientious Objectors. At this time she lived with her lover, Eleanor Rogers, but Butts was rarely faithful to one partner, and the relationships she had during her lifetime frequently overlapped. She was also developing a relationship with the Jewish writer and publisher, John Rodker. Eleanor Rogers was aware of Butts' infidelity and it was the cause of frequent bouts of domestic violence. Butts finally left Rogers and married Rodker in 1918. Their daughter Camilla (and

Butts' only child) was born in 1920, just as the marriage was disintegrating. Butts and Rodker separated soon after, and finally divorced in 1927. Butts was never really adept at motherhood and fostered her daughter Camilla out from a very early age. Camilla was never to live with her mother and spent very little time with her, being raised instead by her great aunt.

From London, Butts moved to Paris, spending much of the 1920s moving between the two. She moved in literary circles and was very well connected to other Modernist writers such as HD (Hilda Doolittle), Ezra Pound and Ford Madox Ford. Her work did receive critical acclaim at this time and was said to have also influenced those writers she knew and interacted with, but Leonard and Virginia Woolf at Hogarth Press rejected it. Butts was a long-time drug user, having been addicted to opiates for many years. She was later to inspire Crowley when he wrote *Diary of a Drug Fiend*, and her addiction continued right up to the time of her death.

Butts had a series of relationships with people such as the American composer Virgil Thompson, the French writer Mireille Havet, the Scottish writer and magical practitioner Cecil Maitland (who is considered by some to be the love of her life), and the painter Gabriel Aitkin, whom she married in 1930. After she married Aitkin, they moved to Sennen Cove in Cornwall in 1932, where Butts lived out the rest of her short life. The marriage ended in 1934, and Butts died suddenly in 1937. She developed a stomach ulcer, which was perforated during surgery, and she died of peritonitis at the age of forty six. She was buried in the local churchyard in Sennen.

At her death, Butts' daughter Camilla became her literary executor, but she was reluctant to part with her mother's papers. Despite repeated requests from Yale University, she held onto them as she felt she wanted to get to know her mother better and she believed her papers were the means by which she could do this. The papers remained private until relatively recently, at which point Camilla allowed Nathalie Blondel to have access. This is thought to be one of the reasons why Butts' work remained so obscure for so many years, in terms of the literary canon, as scholars were unable to examine Butts' oeuvre until relatively recently. This stifled any debate that may have taken place around her work, and effectively silenced Butts.

Butts and Spirituality (and Politics)

There is little doubt that Butts had an active spiritual life and according to her principle biographer, Nathalie Blondel, she also studied the occult throughout her 20s, undergoing two separate initiations. One was by Phillip Hesseltine (a.k.a. Peter Warlock), a British composer and occultist, who was friends with both D.H. Lawrence and W.B. Yeats. The second was with Aleister Crowley. In June 1921, Butts travelled with Cecil Maitland to stay with Crowley in Sicily, where he was working on *Book Four*. Butts became one of his collaborative students and Crowley credited her as having been of great use while they were working on the third part of the book, *Magick in Theory and Practice*. In later editions, such as the 1994 edition introduced by Hymenaeus Beta, she is credited as a co-writer alongside Mary Desti and Leila Waddel.

However, having spent time with Crowley, Butts rejected this form of magical life and preferred to pursue a simpler path through her own writing. She believed her own path to magical work was to be accessed through her poetry and other writing, and experimented extensively with automatic writing. Her own path, away from the more formal confines of Thelema, was one that was deeply connected to the land, and was deeply influenced by the theories of the Cambridge Ritualists, in particular the work of the classical scholar and anthropologist Jane Harrison, who examined the links between Hellenic traditions and a supposed indigenous British Pre-Christian pagan tradition. Harrison proposed that goddess worship preceded notions of a male god and this linked in to the work of other scholars such as Fraser, who wrote *The Golden Bough*. Butts took Harrison's ideas of a Hellenic past and wove notions of a matriarchal tradition into her own work, which centred on a matrilineal inheritance of, and connection to, the land. She also believed that retaining this spiritual link to the land could heal a sickened soul. As Mary Butts' initial connection was with the Dorset countryside, this became the benchmark against which every other landscape was measured. The landscapes she loved the best were ones that were reminiscent of the coastline around Salterns, such as Sennen Cove, where she finally settled and was buried. But it is Butts' link to the land, and her philosophies on the supposed entitlement to that link, that give us the most controversial areas of Butts' work.

In 1932 Butts published an article, entitled 'Warning to Hikers' in which she sets out her beliefs around moral and spiritual rights to the land. In the 1930s, England was enjoying a countryside revival and the most fashionable pursuit for the city dweller was to spend time in the country at weekends. It was at this time that Mary Webb also enjoyed posthumous popularity and the well-known Michelin Guides to the counties were being published. But it was this popularity of the countryside that Butts spoke so vociferously against. She spoke out against the 'cultural trespass' of the vulgar working class 'anti-citizens', the urban industrial workers who encroached upon the land in their spare time. Butts states that she was 'living in a country where people have lost their stations and like badly-trained children can neither keep to their places or respect other peoples'. So it was not just the non-English who dismayed Butts, there was also a problem with class boundaries. She believed that the urban weekend hiker was committing a bogus sacramental act by forgetting their place in society and believing thoughts of 'unnatural equality'. They were misguidedly demanding access to the land, which the landed gentry had a genuine right to by way of their heredity. Urban trippers, Butts states, defiled the sacred landscape and 'either destroy what they find or are lost in it'. Butts then goes on to suggest that England was being compromised as a result of inter-breeding. The formerly 'pure' man has become polluted, diseased and is now 'leaving a dirty little trail through [nature's] sanctuary'. The scholar Jane Garrity writes that, 'by grouping the concepts of birth right and whiteness with that of England, and in turn by suggesting that these overlapping categories are grounded in the mystical, Butts conveys that the countryman embodies a collective destiny whose essential components are racial health and purity.' While such beliefs may have been more common at the time than we may be comfortable with now (both on the left and right of the political spectrum) history was to show in the next decades the consequences of the far right taking similar ideas of racial purity and white superiority from an ideological to a practical application.

The themes that run through Butts' work as a consequence of these beliefs are that the urban landscape is a wasteland, dominated by science and lack of feeling, which is threatening to engulf the supernatural order of the rural. She is also preoc-cupied with notions of heredity, possibly as a result of her own experiences with Salterns. According to Garrity, Butts places the identification of race and nationhood in the soil of the land. In theory this is all well and good, but the flip side of this philosophy is that it always creates a notion of 'other', or more specifically, the outsider, and questions arise regarding birth right and the movement of populations (or lack of). In Butts' work, characters who are considered 'other' are frequently placed within the narrative, and Butts even suggests that those 'others' are nothing more than a pollutant, a blot on the English landscape. For instance, Garrity notes that in *Armed With Madness* the pollutant is a black gay man, while in *Death of Felicity Taverner* it is a Jewish male communist who represents this unwanted and undesirable other. This does not necessarily mean that Butts did not appreciate other or indigenous cultures; but in her worldview everyone should stay in their place. But trying to unravel this deeply flawed thought process is pointless. If she lived today we would say she was deeply prejudiced and ignorant of diversity.

The effect of these belief systems may not necessarily colour our appreciation or diminish Butts' contribution as an innovative writer, occultist and as a woman living her life on her own terms at a time when women were expected to conform to society's expectations; nevertheless, it is something to be mindful of.

Butts' Written Work

Hailing from Dorset, just like Thomas Hardy, it is no surprise that scholars often draw parallels between Butts' work and that of Thomas Hardy, who Andrew Radford denotes as Butts' 'more renowned literary precursor'. Indeed, Butts herself was openly influenced by the work of Hardy, and considered herself to be an 'imaginative archaeologist', just as Hardy was, recording rural life in her work. However, Butts' vision of the Wessex countryside is quite different to Hardy's, both in terms of politics and class. Unlike those of Hardy, Butts' heroines are not working class women, but those born into the landed upper classes. Being influenced by Jane Harrison and her ideas of a matrilineal link to the land, Butts' women take on the role of priestess, serving the goddess of the land.

Ashe of Rings, which was published in 1925, contains just such themes, and echoes the themes that recurred in Butts' own life. The book follows the Ashe family that live at 'Rings', a house that sits in the shadows of ancient earthworks, the Rings themselves. Throughout the novel, both the house and the barrow are interchangeably referred to as 'Rings', which means it is never quite clear to which Butts is referring. Both house and barrow are therefore interchangeable and synonymous with each other. Stewardship of the house and the pre-historic site sits with the family; 'The head of the family was the guardian of the Rings,' Butts writes. Anthony Ashe, the current guardian when the story opens, must marry and produce a child in order to ensure the future guardianship of Rings. He marries a local girl, Melitta, but she has little or no insight into the role of the women in the family, and even less interest. She knows she must produce children, but has no sense of the sacredness of the land. She has a daughter, but once the girl is born, Melitta does not really take to motherhood, but is determined to retain her place as mistress of Rings. She is interested in the material and social benefits only. Anthony, meanwhile, sets to work on raising the child to be ready to take her place as head of the household, priestess and guardian of Rings. To Anthony, Christianity is just one religious path of many in the world:

> Christianity is a way, a set of symbols, in part to explain and to make men endure, the unutterable pain that is in the world. There are other sets, like chessmen. But only one game.

Instead of a christening, the child is named in a pagan ceremony in the grounds of the house, where a candle is held above her forehead, while a bowl of water and a jar of earth are placed either side of her.

'That is how we christen them at Rings,' Anthony Ashe states. 'Earth and water and fire... Breathe on her then with your maternal breath,' he intones. The girl is named Vanna, and it is her story that the rest of the novel follows, as she loses her father and is exiled from Rings. She must endure trials and much pain before she is restored to her place as guardian.

As with our other writers in this series, Butts' descriptions of Rings and the Wessex countryside are particularly lovely, and are filled with a sense of the numinous. There is also a strong sense of animism, and the house at Rings takes on an animal-like quality.

In the summer the house swooned; in winter it slept like a bear. Through the afternoons it could be heard, sucking in its sleep, milky draughts, bubbles of quiet, drunk against the future when it should become a wrath. On spring nights there became imminent the fantasy of Rings; when, on the screaming wind, the Rings went sailing, and hovered over the house and swooped and fanned, and skimmed away in the dark, a cap between the roof and the blazing stars.

This at the equinox. At the solstice there was a calm, a quiet of the siren's sea. The sun that obliterates all shadows and the sun that darkens them laid their gilt fingers across the empty rooms. The dust rose. Between the light rods, specks danced and Rings showed its teeth.

This animism also extends to the Wessex countryside, and Butts' descriptions of nature are similarly filled with a sense of the mystical.

That night the moon climbed over Rings. A bodiless shadow whipped round the barrow and skipped on its pale cone. The faintly clashing boughs accompanied it, and ceased as it darted into their shadows. To a light clapping it spun out, to reel and trip over a moon shaft, and gather and prick the earth, and stab, and stab...

In the centre of the wood there was a large stone. It sucked the moon's white and gave back its own, a great egg at the point of cracking, so smooth, so blank.

The shadow flickered and darted deeper into the heart of the trees.

As well as Butts' novels, essays and short stories, she was also the keeper of a journal from the time when she was in her twenties. Bearing in mind the circles she moved in, and her obvious fascination with magic and the occult, this in itself makes for fascinating reading. What is clear, from both Butts' writing and from the way in which she lived her life, despite her questionable political ideas, she was a woman who lived life on her own terms, and was not to be swayed by the expectations or pressures of society. This in itself makes her a fascinating writer to delve into.

J.R.R. Tolkien (1892 – 1973)

Unlike any of our other Nature Mystics in this series, J.R.R. Tolkien was a devout Catholic, and remained so all of his life. So what is Tolkien doing in a book that looks at the roots of Modern Paganism in literature? Tolkien holds a unique status among modern writers, in that both Christians and Modern Pagans alike try to claim him as their own. A brief search of the Internet will uncover scores of articles all stating cases for how his work alludes to their own belief systems in the subtext of his plots. For instance, from evangelical Christians, to Catholics, to Druids and Wiccans, there are cases presented for how the story of the fallen hero who is resurrected becomes an allegory for the fallen god-figure who is later raised from the dead. Rather than join this chorus of voices, this chapter will not try to tease out the pagan mythology embedded in *The Hobbit* or *The Lord of the Rings*, instead I will examine some of the elements that put Tolkien high on most Modern Pagans' lists of favourite reading material. Just what is it about Tolkien that appeals to us?

Tolkien was essentially both a conservationist and a linguist; he cared passionately about the preservation of the countryside, and his first love was languages: how they are constructed, and how they survive over time. He himself spoke many different languages (Latin, French, German, Middle English, Old English, Finnish, Gothic, Greek, Italian, Old Norse, Spanish, Welsh, Medieval Welsh, Danish, Dutch, Lombardic, Norwegian, Russian, Serbian, and Swedish to be precise). These elements of philology and conservationism were woven into his fiction writing, as well as his daily life; but he also had a strong belief in the importance of folklore to the life of a living language. For him, artificially constructed languages like Esperanto were inevitably destined to failure as they had not developed a corresponding body of mythology. As a counterpoint, Tolkien developed fully formed languages like Elvish, and a comprehensive body of folklore, mythology and cartography to support it, all woven around Middle Earth. This went a step further than most fantasy fiction, and set the bar for writers who followed after him. It also helps to separate out quality fantasy fiction from the Tolkien 'wannabes' who pale in comparison, as they lack the depth of detail of Tolkien. These are the elements that have gone on to be an inspiration for so many generations of counter-culture readers.

Tolkien's Life: Putting His Work in Context

John Ronald Reuel Tolkien was born in 1892 in Bloemfontein in the Orange Free State of South Africa. While the family name was German or Prussian in origin, Tolkien's parents were English, and had left England when his father was promoted to manager at the Bloemfontein office of the British bank he worked for. Tolkien had one younger brother, Hilary. When he was three, his mother (Mabel) took the boys on what was intended to be an extended family visit to England, but before he could join them, Tolkien's father died of rheumatic fever in South Africa. This left Mabel without husband or income, so she took the boys to live with her parents in King's Heath, Birmingham. In 1896 they moved to Sarehole, just outside Birmingham, and the young Tolkien enjoyed exploring the local countryside around the Lickey and Malvern Hills, as well as visiting his Aunt Jane's farm at Bag End. These landscapes were to be reflected in his written work. Mabel educated the two boys at home, and John quickly developed an interest in botany, as well as drawing landscapes and trees. However, his favourite lessons were in languages, and he soon learnt the basics of Latin. Their peaceful life was cut short in 1904 when Mabel died of acute diabetes at the age of thirty four, almost two decades before the discovery of insulin. Before her death, Mabel had entrusted the upbringing of her boys to Brother Francis Xavier Morgan of the Birmingham

Oratory, who was required to bring them up as good Catholics. Father Morgan was to have a lasting influence on both boys, and took them to live in Edgbaston.

Tolkien's first foray into a constructed language was that of Animalic, an invention of his cousins. At this time, Tolkien was in his teens, and was absorbed in studying both Latin and Anglo Saxon. Soon after, he started experimenting with his own languages – his fascination had been sparked, and was to stay with him for the rest of his life. It was at King Edward's School in Birmingham that Tolkien was to develop a potent love of poetry, which also formed an important part of his written work later in life. A trip to Switzerland in 1911 proved to be very influential: Tolkien trekked across the mountains, a journey that was later to be reflected in Bilbo's journey across the Misty Mountains. Later that year, Tolkien began studying classics at Exeter College, Oxford, but later changed his degree to one in English language and literature. This was to be the start of his academic career, which ran alongside his writing.

At the age of sixteen, Tolkien met Edith Bratt, who was three years his senior, when he and his brother moved into the boarding house where Edith lived. They quickly struck up a bond, and enjoyed frequenting a Birmingham teashop that had a balcony overlooking the pavement. From here Edith and Tolkien liked to sit and throw sugar lumps onto the hats of the unsuspecting passers-by underneath them. However, their emerging relationship was a concern to his guardian, who was concerned about Edith's Protestantism; he felt the relationship had affected Tolkien's exam results, and he forbade the young lovers from having any further contact until Tolkien reached the age of twenty one. If Tolkien did not stop, his university career would be cut short. Tolkien wrote a letter to his son, Michael, many years later that explained the situation, in which he stated: 'For very nearly three years I did not see or write to my lover. It was extremely hard, especially at first. The effects were not wholly good: I fell back into folly and slackness and misspent a good deal of my first year at college.' On the day of his twenty-first birthday, Tolkien wrote to Edith and told her that he had never stopped loving her, and that he wanted to marry her. They met again for the first time in 1913, when Edith accepted his proposal. Edith converted to Catholicism, and they were married in 1916. The marriage was a very successful one, and the couple went on to have four children, of whom one, Christopher, was responsible for ensuring the entire body of Tolkien's work was published, some of it posthumously. Tolkien was dedicated to his family life, and many of his works (such as *The Hobbit*) started out as stories he wrote for his children.

In 1914, with the outbreak of war, Tolkien did not immediately enlist. Instead he chose to enter a programme that would allow him to complete his degree studies before joining the army. Despite public pressure for all young men to enlist straightaway, Tolkien completed his studies in 1915, and was then trained and commissioned to the British Expeditionary Force, and was sent to France in 1916. Expecting to join the thousands of young men who were killed very quickly in the Somme, it was an anxious time for Tolkien and Edith, but they were able to bypass the Army's postal censorship by writing letters in code. This way, Edith was able to trace Tolkien's movements across the Western Front. In October 1916, Tolkien was taken down with Trench Fever, a common illness spread by the poor conditions and profusion of lice in the trenches. He was sent home to England as an invalid, just before most of his battalion were wiped out in the fighting. Tolkien was then deemed medically unfit for active duty, and spent the remainder of the war in recovery, or assigned to garrison duties. It was at this time that he started work writing his first fiction, starting with 'The Fall of Gondolin'. Although many theories have suggested that Tolkien was heavily influenced by his wartime experiences while writing *The Lord of the Rings*, he steadfastly refuted this theory.

Following the end of the war in 1918, Tolkien's first civilian job was working at the Oxford English Dictionary, and then in 1920, he took up his post as a Reader of English Language at the University of Leeds, where he became their youngest professor. He began to translate works such as *Sir Gawain and the Green Knight*, before returning to Oxford in 1925 as a Professor of Anglo-Saxon at Pembroke College. It was here that he wrote *The Hobbit*, and the first two volumes of *The Lord of the Rings*. Between 1920 and 1926, Tolkien worked on a translation of *Beowulf*, which was finally published in 2014, almost ninety years after its completion, and his work has had a lasting effect on *Beowulf* readers, as it established the poetic nature of the work. Tolkien also acknowledged that this work was 'among my most valued sources' when constructing Middle Earth. Years later W.H. Auden, a student of Tolkien's, recalled a *Beowulf* lecture which Tolkien began with a dramatic reading of the text in Anglo-Saxon, in what Auden described as 'the voice of Gandalf'. During his years in Oxford, Tolkien also became a member of The Inklings, an informal group of men that met regularly to discuss and read their unfinished literary work. Among the other Inklings was C.S. Lewis, whom Tolkien befriended, and is credited as having converted from Atheism to Christianity (although Tolkien experienced a degree of consternation when Lewis chose Anglicanism instead of Catholicism).

As the Second World War approached, Tolkien volunteered as both a code-breaker and a cartographer, but he never saw active duty. This allowed his written work to continue uninterrupted. In 1945, he moved to Merton College as a Professor of English Language and Literature. Here, he completed *The Lord of the Rings* in 1945. In 1959, Tolkien retired from academic life. Alarmed by the popularity of his books amongst those involved in the counter-culture movement in the 1960s, he and Edith moved to Bournemouth to escape some of the public attention and literary fame he had gained. When Edith died in 1971 at the age of eighty-two, Tolkien buried her in Oxford, and had the name 'Luthien' engraved on her tombstone (Luthien, in the folklore of Middle Earth, was the most beautiful elf, who sacrificed her immortality for her love of the mortal warrior Beren). Tolkien returned to rooms at Merton College, but died two years later in at the age of eighty one. He was buried with Edith, and beneath his name on their tombstone, was carved the name 'Beren'.

Tolkien, Politics and Spirituality

According to Ronald Hutton in *The Triumph of the Moon*, Modern Paganism developed from a range of movements in late Victorian and early twentieth century society. One of those forces was literature, another was the late Victorian revival of folklore, and a third element was the Countryside Revival of the 1930s and 1940s. In Tolkien's work we can see a melting pot for all of those cultural foundations, which is why, I believe, Tolkien stands alongside our other Nature Mystics as one of the creative forces that shaped Modern Paganism as it is today. It is also why counter-culture movements, from the hippies in the 1960s to the 'Boys in Black' and the live-action role-players (Larpers) that exist within the Modern Paganism that we know currently, are all drawn to Tolkien's work.

As mentioned previously, Tolkien was a devout Catholic by upbringing, and while this belief system was an important anchor throughout his life, he was adamant that neither his religious beliefs nor any other personal experiences made their way into his written work. To confirm this, in his introduction to *The Lord of the Rings*, Tolkien adamantly states that, 'As for any inner meaning or 'message', it has in the intention of the author none. It is neither allegorical nor topical,' meaning that he did not intend it to be in any way representative of his own beliefs or experiences. Of course, it is possible to argue that some element will have come through unconsciously, but we can only take

Tolkien's word for this. As part of the Inklings' discussions, Tolkien was also was highly critical of C.S. Lewis for his overt allegorical use of Christian themes. Tolkien was very traditional in his Catholicism. He did not hold with modernization of the church, and, when the Catholic Church started to make changes (such as saying the Liturgy in English) Tolkien was fiercely against them. Tolkien's grandson remembers his childhood embarrassment at standing alongside Tolkien in church and hearing his elderly grandfather steadfastly responding very loudly to the Liturgy in Latin.

Despite Tolkien's clear religious affiliations, there are a number of different areas in which we begin to see more obvious parallels with the Modern Pagan sensibility. In this section, I will tease out some of those similarities. Although a more traditional definition of 'religious' beliefs may view political and religious beliefs as two very separate entities, there is a distinct difference between 'religious affiliation' and a 'spiritual life'. Modern Paganism encourages a much wider scope for what constitutes a spiritual path, and Modern Pagans often include their work, their political affiliations and their creative endeavours within their spiritual life. There is a sense that our whole lives are lived as a demonstration of our relationship with the divine, instead of just the time spent in active worship. I will, therefore, take some poetic license, and expand beyond Tolkien's Catholicism, to explore something of his interest in mythology, the role of the writer, as well as his interest in conservation, and his political views.

With regards to mythology and the role of the writer, Tolkien was one of a group of people who believe that mythology holds clues to a universal divine 'truth' and that if we wish to uncover divine truths, we must look to mythology to do this. As part of this, the writer's role in producing poetry or mythology, therefore, is divinely inspired. Writing from a pagan perspective, this holds a lot of parallels with my own belief system, although the shape of that god might be different. The source of creativity (for me) is something that is deeply personal, and tied irrevocably to my spiritual path. It was in this way that for Tolkien, language and mythology were very much tied up with the writer's relationship to the divine also, and also with the concept of cultural identity. Post-colonial theorists have written many papers on the links between cultural identity and language, and how severing a people from their own language can have catastrophic consequences. Similarly, Tolkien believed that in order for a language to survive, it had to hold cultural resonance for people, and, that cultural resonance is secured by the existence of a corresponding body of folklore. Tolkien's own work on Middle Earth and its languages, such as Elvish, are startling in the level of detail that he included. Tolkien did not just construct an empty language for fictional purposes; he constructed an alphabet, a cartography, a mythology, and a group (albeit fictional) of people with a strong sense of identity of their own. This is what enables Middle Earth be so compelling for generations of readers of every faith.

Tolkien has been criticized over the years for some questionable beliefs that are allegedly to be found in his work. For example, some critics suggest that Tolkien's work demonstrates racist views, because of the association of good and evil (in a very literal way, because the Morgul Lords are always referred to as the 'Black Riders' and most of the associations of evil are with darkness of colour). To reach an understanding of this, one has to return to how Tolkien lived his own life as a demonstration of his beliefs. For a man with a Germanic name like Tolkien in the inter-war period, life in England wouldn't have been straightforward. Anti-German propaganda was prevalent, with the British press choosing to stir up anti-German feeling amongst the population. (It was only in 1917 that the British Royal Family bowed to public opinion and changed their family name from the Germanic Saxe-Coburg to Windsor).

Tolkien was very vocal in his rejection of such discriminatory beliefs on all sides, and his rejection of prejudice also extended to a refusal of Germany's own racist policies. As *The Hobbit* was being prepared for publication in Nazi Germany in 1938, to Tolkien's horror, he was asked to comment on whether or not he was of Aryan origin. Tolkien's response was to declare that the Nazi 'race-doctrine' was 'wholly pernicious and unscientific'. He then wrote to the publisher and stated that if what they were really asking was if he was of Jewish origin, 'I can only reply that I regret that I appear to have no ancestors of that gifted people'. Tolkien was equally as vocal about his horror of how people of different racial backgrounds were treated in other countries, for example, the racial segregation in South Africa, where he was born. If any racist elements are to be found in Tolkien's written work, it is most likely that these are unintentional, and are a reflection of the fact that (by our standards today) Britain in the earlier part of the twentieth century was not as aware of diversity and inequality as we are now. He may have an unconscious euro-centric bias in his work, but there is a logic to this when we recall that Tolkien's area of research was Anglo-Saxon, old-English and Norse languages and culture. This was the area he knew the most about.

Another area of Tolkien's political beliefs that overlaps with a Modern Pagan worldview of spirituality, is his strong sense of conservation. For many years Tolkien refused even to own a car, instead preferring the bicycle as his chosen method of transport, and he was very vocal about his dislike of industrialization, which was destroying the English countryside and making life far more complicated than it needed to be. This viewpoint is evident in the portrayal of the Shire, before and after Saruman's intervention. Before forced industrialization, the Shire is an idyllic place, and life there is peaceful, simple and slow, almost to the point of frustration. Before he is compelled to go on his adventures with the Ring, Frodo says to Gandalf:

I should like to save the Shire, if I could – though there have been times when I thought the inhabitants too stupid and dull for words, and have felt that an earthquake or an invasion of dragons might be good for them. But I don't feel like that now. I feel that as long as the Shire lies behind, safe and comfortable, I shall find wandering more bearable. I shall know that somewhere there is a firm foothold, even if my feet cannot stand there again.

For Frodo (and perhaps for Tolkien and the rest of us) the risk of 'stepping onto a road' and being taken away from Bag End is one of exile. This is not merely a holiday Frodo is going on; the journey will be perilous and he does not know if he will return. However, like many people faced with exile, Frodo finds comfort in knowing that the Shire is still there, preserved as it always was. The prospect of the future homecoming of the hobbits is somewhat tainted, however, when Sam gazes into the Mirror of Galadriel. He is given a foretaste of what will later happen to the Shire, as he sees the wholescale felling of trees, and chimneys belching out black smoke. It is almost enough to turn him aside from his path, and only his loyalty to Frodo keeps him from returning straight away.

Like a dream the vision shifted and went back, and he saw the trees again. But this time they were not so close, and he could see what was going on: they were not waving in the wind, they were falling, crashing to the ground.

'Hi!' cried Sam in an outraged voice. 'There's that Ted Sandyman a-cutting down trees as he shouldn't. They didn't ought to be felled: it's that avenue beyond the Mill that shades the road to Bywater. I wish I could get at Ted, and I'd fell him!'

But now Sam noticed that the Old Mill had vanished, and a large red-brick building was being put up where it had stood. Lots of folk were busily at work. There was a tall red chimney nearby.

Black smoke seemed to cloud the surface of the Mirror.

'There's some devilry at work in the Shire,' he said.

In Sam's view of the world, industrialization immediately becomes associated with 'devilry at work'. When he and the other hobbits return to the Shire after their adventures have concluded, the vision they are met with is just as bad as the premonition that Sam saw in Galadriel's mirror. When the hobbits finally return home, they discover that Saruman has taken over the Shire and destroyed much of its natural beauty; they are faced with further dilemmas and they must set to work. Once they have overthrown Saruman, the task of restoring the Shire to its original state must begin, aided by the box of Elven earth that Galadriel gifted Sam with.

While Tolkien's own spiritual beliefs took him down a very traditional path, one that is not obviously connected in any way with pagan beliefs, it is possible to see that his cultural under-standing of a wider society bears much in common with more modern outlooks. It is also worth noting that Middle Earth was not a society that had been converted to Christianity, but instead belonged to a time of 'virtuous paganism', where the inhabitants lived good and virtuous lives without the moral framework of the church.

Tolkien's Written Work

During Tolkien's long academic and writing career, he worked on many books that are well worth exploring. At one end of his scale, his children's books are delightful. *The Hobbit* was written for Tolkien's children, and this was not the only work he wrote for them. He also wrote a series of letters from Father Christmas, which he built up over many years. Each year the cast of characters would get more and more complex; this was one of the books published posthumously by his son, Christopher, as *The Father Christmas Letters*. He also expanded some of the stories of the characters touched upon in his more well-known works, which were also later published, such as *The Adventures of Tom Bombadil* and *Farmer Giles of Ham*. At the other end of the scale, some of his more academic works have also gone on to become authoritative texts in their field, such as his translation of *Beowulf*. Also worthy of mention is *The Silmarillion*, his mythopoeic work which covered the legends of Middle Earth, such as Beren and Luthien, and Turin. While *The Silmarillion* was not published in his lifetime, as Tolkien's publisher got cold feet (and the cost of publishing at that time meant they were very cautious about what was worth investing in), both *The Silmarillion* and *Beowulf* became significant influences on *The Hobbit* and *The Lord of the Rings*, which are of course Tolkien's most famous works, and arguably his most well-rounded. *Beowulf* sparked Tolkien's interest in monsters in fiction, most famously the dragon in *Beowulf* which then went on to influence the creation of Smaug, and the Elvish folklore explored in *The Silmarillion* became the basis of his later works, and the stories were woven in to the stories of the hobbits.

The success of Tolkien's writing career started (like that of many writers) accidentally, when *The Hobbit* came to the attention of a publisher in 1936. Tolkien never expected the book to be successful; however, it sold enough copies to compel the publisher to encourage Tolkien to write a sequel. It was this sequel, published originally in three volumes, that was to change the face of fiction writing, and influence the genre of fantasy fiction which has followed close on its heels. *The Lord of the Rings* was intended to be children's literature to begin with, but the story very quickly took on much darker qualities, and since *The Hobbit* had had as big a readership among adults as it did among children, making the switch to adult fiction was simple. What is so unique about *The Lord of the Rings* is that it has maintained its popularity ever since it was published, and has never really left the best-sellers' lists since then. As most of our Nature Mystics have shown, it is often more common for books to go through periods of popularity followed by periods of obscurity. Undoubtedly, this has been helped along by the adaptations that have followed, such as the BBC Radio 4 production developed by Brian Sibley in the 1980s, and the Peter Jackson films. In his own lifetime, Tolkien was frequently disapproving of artistic representations of his work, as he believed that fantasy was best left to literature, and not to drama, which he considered 'naturally hostile to Fantasy'. On receiving one proposed screenplay, Tolkien responded by saying it had treated his work 'carelessly in general, in places recklessly, and with no evident signs of any appreciation of what it is all about'. Needless to say, the adaptations that we know and love today were not undertaken until much later, and although Tolkien himself may have disapproved, they have undoubtedly brought his works to the attention of another generation of readers.

The radio production also had another benefit, which is often overlooked: the setting of some of Tolkien's poems from *The Lord of the Rings* to music, thereby creating folk songs which form a vital element to the Middle Earth mythology. Most notable were Bilbo's song, 'The Road Goes Ever On and On', and Sam's rendition of 'Gil-galad was an Elven King' which he sings to the company on the journey to Weathertop. When they reach Weathertop, the company asks Strider to tell them more of the story, but Strider suggests that the tale of Gil-galad is not appropriate for where they are, and instead tells them the tale of Beren and Luthien (Tinuviel in Elvish), which Tolkien was to associate with himself and his wife:

'I will tell you the tale of Tinúviel,' said Strider, 'in brief – for it is a long tale of which the end is not known; and there are none now, except Elrond, that remember it aright as it was told of old. It is a fair tale, though it is sad, as are all the tales of Middle-earth, and yet it may lift up your hearts.' He was silent for some time, and then he began not to speak but to chant softly:

The leaves were long, the grass was green,
The hemlock-umbels tall and fair,
And in the glade a light was seen
Of stars in shadow shimmering.
Tinúviel was dancing there
To music of a pipe unseen,
And light of stars was in her hair,
And in her raiment glimmering.

There Beren came from mountains cold,
And lost he wandered under leaves,
And where the Elven-river rolled
He walked alone and sorrowing.
He peered between the hemlock-leaves
And saw in wander flowers of gold
Upon her mantle and her sleeves,
And her hair like shadow following.

Enchantment healed his weary feet
That over hills were doomed to roam;
And forth he hastened, strong and fleet,
And grasped at moonbeams glistening.
Through woven woods in Elvenhome
She tightly fled on dancing feet,
And left him lonely still to roam
In the silent forest listening.

In effect, the characters of Bilbo, Frodo and Aragorn take on the mantle of the folklorist by translating and writing down the folk tales and songs from the Elvish into the 'common tongue', spoken by hobbits and men. This preserves the body of folklore, and ensures it will not be forgotten when the Elves pass into the West, much as Victorian and early twentieth century folklorists were preserving traditional tales and songs in Tolkien's time. It is the interweaving of the maps, the languages, the poetry and its corresponding body of folklore that makes the world of Middle Earth so compelling and appeals to readers of the pagan community. I believe that this is what makes this series of books so crucial to any investigation into key 'pagan' texts, irrespective of the belief system of its author.

E. Nesbit (1858 – 1924)

Edith Nesbit is certainly one of the more eccentric of our Nature Mystics, and one of the most fascinating for students of esoterica, particularly those interested by the Western Mystery Tradition. Best known for her children's novels *The Railway Children, The Story of the Treasure Seekers* and *Five Children and It,* Nesbit wrote more than forty novels for adults and children, and co-authored many more. But it is not just her written work that made Nesbit influential; she was also a member of two of the most significant societies of the late nineteenth and early twentieth centuries. Her political interests led her to be a co-founder of the Fabian Society and she was also a member of the Hermetic Order of the Golden Dawn. Although the influence of the Fabian Society may appear only hazily through the mists of history, the society was concerned with socialist interests (it later became associated with the Labour Party) and members of the society went on to establish the London School of Economics. It was also instrumental in bringing about the reforms that led to a universal healthcare system and the national minimum wage. Many critics have forged a link between socialist beliefs and an interest in the occult in the late Victorian period, as both interests were often expressed as part of the avant garde rejection of the conventional religion and politics of the era. This certainly seems to have been the case with Nesbit and several of her peers, who shared interests in the Golden Dawn and the Theosophical Society. There is no doubt, however, that between the Golden Dawn and the Fabian Society Nesbit moved in distinguished circles.

Her private life is where Nesbit's story becomes even more intriguing. Married to a serial philanderer at the age of eighteen and seven months' pregnant, Nesbit had to 'share' her husband, Hubert Bland, with his many lovers, even living with two of them and adopting Bland's children by his mistress. Later in her marriage, Nesbit herself went on to find consolation by taking younger lovers of her own, possibly including George Bernard Shaw.

But setting personal and political life aside, just how far do Nesbit's esoteric interests come out in her children's books? If we examine the more run-of-the-mill children's books (like *The Railway Children*), the answer might be 'not much'; however, Nesbit made forays into magical realism that carry the full weight of her Golden Dawn associations. This chapter will look at two of her books, *The Accidental Magic*, and *The Amulet*, which was the third in her trilogy of books to return to the story of the Psammead from the *Five Children and It* series.

Nesbit's Life: Putting Her Work in Context

Nesbit was born in 1858 in Kennington. Her father, an agricultural chemist, died when Nesbit was four years old, leaving her mother to bring up their two daughters alone. Nesbit's sister, Mary, suffered from ill health, so much of Edith's childhood was spent in travelling around Europe, largely in France, Spain and Germany. During Edith's fourteenth year, the family returned to England, and settled in Halstead, Kent, which was thought to have inspired *The Railway Children*. Nesbit's childhood clearly had a significant influence on her, as many of her plots involve an absent father, and a mother who must battle ill-health, relative poverty and misfortune to hold the family together.

At seventeen, the family returned to London, and it was here that Edith met Hubert Bland, and fell pregnant. The couple married in April 1880, but did not immediately live together. To begin with, Bland stated a preference to remain living with his mother, but the real reason soon became apparent, when Edith discovered that his mother's paid companion, Maggie Doran, also lived in the house and she too was pregnant with Bland's child. In a somewhat bizarre relationship, this pattern was set to continue for several years, with Bland splitting his time between

Nesbit and Doran, even after Nesbit became aware of the arrangement. Living alone with a young child and having to be financially independent, Nesbit started to earn a living through selling her stories and poems, and the composition of greetings cards.

When the couple did finally share a marital home, it too became an unconventional household. When Edith's close friend, Alice Hoatson had been asked to distract Bland from his most recent lover, she too fell under Bland's spell. Hoatson gave birth to her first child with Bland, Rosamund, in 1886, and the child was then adopted by Nesbit. Alice moved into the Bland household to act as secretary and housekeeper, and thirteen years later, she gave birth to Bland's second child. Nesbit again became the adopted mother. To the outside world the Blands were an ordinary family, but behind closed doors things were very different. Hoatson and Nesbit agreed that they must keep up a very conventional public front, as to be exposed would threaten both Bland and Nesbit's writing careers, so they maintained the subterfuge to all except their closest friends. Between Hoatson and Nesbit, the family had a total of five children: Paul (to whom *The Railway Children* was dedicated), Iris, Fabian, Rosamund, and John. However, despite the number of children in the household, Nesbit was sometimes ambivalent about motherhood; there was no doubt that she loved her children deeply, but she was also once quoted as saying that children were something that one poured a lot of love into, but received very little in return. The family doesn't appear to have been an especially nurturing household, and was not without its tragedies: Nesbit's son Fabian (to whom a number of Nesbit's books were dedicated and who was named after the society) died at the age of fifteen following a tonsillectomy, as the adult members of the household had neglected to tell him not to eat prior to his operation. He reacted badly to the anaesthetic, and choked on his own vomit.

Towards the end of her twenties, Nesbit began her own string of affairs, largely with younger men. She is described as having been a striking figure in London society. She smoked incessantly, went everywhere with a long cigarette holder, and was more often than not surrounded by a coterie of adoring young men. Nesbit was tall, and magnificent in appearance. Her most famous lover was George Bernard Shaw, a fellow Fabian, to whom she remained closely tied until the end of her life. Shaw and Nesbit embarked on a passionate affair, but one that was unconsummated. It is possible that Shaw had not come to terms with his own sexuality, as he had a reputation for only pursuing women who could not accept his proposals, and his own marriage lasted forty one years without being consummated. Although Nesbit seriously considered leaving Bland at this point, she remained in her own marriage, but Shaw remained a strong influence in her life, assisting her financially when she struggled later in life.

It was in her forties that Nesbit's literary career took off. Until then she had always considered herself a poet, but now she turned her hand to children's stories, which were immensely successful. Her own success, and Bland's burgeoning career in journalism, allowed them to move to Well Hall in Eltham, a large moated mansion house. When their financial situation took a dip later, Nesbit took in paying guests and also sold fruit and vegetables she grew in the grounds. The Blands also took in various waifs and strays, including Maggie Doran, the mother of Bland's first illegitimate child; when Doran fell on hard times, she came to live with the Blands and remained there until her early death in 1903.

Despite the highly unusual family dynamics, and the stormy relationship Nesbit had with her husband, the marriage continued until Bland's death in 1914. At about this time, Nesbit's own creativity started to dwindle, and there followed a period of great financial hardship. Three years later, Nesbit married Thomas Tucker, a marine engineer known as 'The Skipper'.

Although they came from different social classes, the couple were very happy together. After thirty one years of living with Nesbit, Alice Hoatson returned to London, and Nesbit and Tucker left Well Hall and moved to St Mary's in the Marsh, where Nesbit befriended a young Noel Coward, who also lived in the village. Nesbit's health was by now severely affected by her incessant smoking, and she suffered repeatedly from bouts of asthma and bronchitis. She died from lung cancer in 1924.

Following Nesbit's death, Alice Hoatson continued the pretence that Nesbit was the biological mother of Rosamund and John, and the family continued to conceal its bohemian roots, but the cracks continued to show. Nesbit's eldest son, Paul, struggled with his family past, and was unhappy in his own marriage, committing suicide in 1940. Rosamund went on to care for Skipper in his final years, and published one novel, before disappearing into obscurity. Nesbit's true legacy was in her writing. As a final postscript, Nesbit's impact on Noel Coward remained with him until the end. When he died, he was found with a copy of Nesbit's *The Enchanted Castle* by his bedside.

Nesbit, Politics and Spirituality

Nesbit's political and spiritual beliefs were very much tied to her affiliations to both The Fabian Society and the Hermetic Order of the Golden Dawn. Nesbit and Bland were both instrumental in establishing The Fabian Society, and its membership was illustrious. Amongst the members were H.G. Wells (another serial philanderer) and his wife Amy, Rebecca West (author of works such as *The Return of the Soldier* and lover of Wells, who herself maintained a very Bohemian family life, giving birth to Wells' son out of wedlock). G.K. Chesterton, Sydney and Beatrice Webb, Eleanor Marx (daughter of Karl Marx) and George Bernard Shaw were also members, as was Annie Besant, who later became the leader of the Theosophical Society. When Nesbit published her breakthrough book, *The Story of the Treasure Seekers* in 1899, the names of the children in the book were taken from Nesbit's coterie of young Fabian men. When H.G. Wells and his wife joined the society in 1903, the Wells and Bland households became very close for several years, with Wells spending much time at Well Hall. However, disagreements as to the running of the Fabian Society came between them, when Wells tried to re-organise the Fabians to become more like a fully-fledged political party. The wedge was driven even deeper when Wells began an affair with Bland's daughter Rosamund and attempted to elope with her in 1908. Hugo Bland caught up with the couple fleeing for Paris at Paddington Station in London, and gave Wells a thorough thrashing. When Wells later got another member of the Fabians (Amber Reeves) pregnant, he left the society in disgrace.

Nesbit drifted away from the Fabian Society when she reached the age of fifty, and instead became absorbed with the Baconian controversy, a group of conspiracy theorists who believed that it was Francis Bacon who wrote all of Shakespeare's plays, as with his apparently restricted education, they reasoned that William Shakespeare could not possibly have written them. Taking the theory one step further, a more esoteric arm of the movement also believed that Bacon had embedded secret ciphers to the Rosicrucian and Masonic mysteries in the plays; if one could uncover the right logarithm, all of the mysteries would be revealed. It was this search for mystical enlightenment that drew Nesbit's attention, and she spent considerable time, effort and money in attempting to uncover those mysteries. This interest in the esoteric mysteries was really a continuation of the interest that had seen Nesbit as an active member of the Hermetic Order of the Golden Dawn, which brought her into contact with the leading esoteric thinkers in London at that time; William Butler Yeats, Maude Gonne, Aleister Crowley, MacGregor Mathers, and Florence Farr, with whom Nesbit had a close friendship for many years. Most of Nesbit's biographers skate over the surface of her interest in the esoteric, but the results of this interest are clearly evident in some of her written work.

As any true Nature Mystic would, Nesbit loved to write in nature, and wrote several of her books whilst sitting in a small rowing boat on the moat at Well Hall.

Nesbit's Written Work

Nesbit's written work was prolific, publishing approximately forty books for children, as well as collaborating on others, and writing poetry and fiction for adults. One of her most recent biographers, Julia Briggs, credits Nesbit with being the first modern writer for children, and her work had a lasting impact on many other well-known authors. Nesbit was the first children's author to write using magical realism; instead of being transported into other magical realms in order for adventures to occur (like Alice in Lewis Carrol's *Wonderland*, or the Darlings in *Peter Pan*), the children in her books would uncover magic in the mundane world. Nesbit wrote real-world children, with real-world problems. They would often uncover magical objects or beings or places in the real world and sometimes these would then lead them to other lands, but principally they were based on real children. Nesbit's work went on to influence many subsequent children's writers, such as Noel Streatfield, C.S. Lewis and J.K. Rowling. More recently, Jacqueline Wilson has written a sequel to the Psammead trilogy. In this section, I will look at two of Nesbit's books that follow this pattern, and examine something of Nesbit's esoteric interests in doing so. The first is *The Accidental Magic* and the second is *The Story of the Amulet*.

The Accidental Magic: Or Don't Tell All You Know (1912) follows the adventures of Quentin de Ward, a 'rather nice little boy' who has not spent much time with other children. Like many of Nesbit's children, Quentin is not quite ordinary, and like Nesbit's other children, his father is away in India, while his mother lives alone in the New Forest. It is not just Quentin's solitude that sets him apart, but also his relationship with his rather extraordinary mother. Mrs de Ward reads a good many books, and then tells Quentin all about them, but her choice of reading is not ordinary; they are 'out of the way books':

> For Mrs de Ward was interested in all the things that people are not quite sure about – the things that are hidden and secret, wonderful and mysterious – the things people make discoveries about. So that when the two were having their tea on the little brick terrace in front of the hollyhocks, with the white cloth flapping in the breeze, and the wasps hovering round the jam-pot, it was no uncommon thing for Quentin to say thickly through his bread and jam, 'I say, mother, tell me some more about Atlantis.' Or, 'Mother tell me some more about Ancient Egypt and the little toy boats they made for their little boys.' Or, 'Mother, tell me about the people who think Lord Bacon wrote Shakespeare'.

This short excerpt clearly reveals Nesbit's own interests, in things that are 'hidden and secret, wonderful and mysterious'. It gives an insight into Nesbit's world of ceremonial magic with the Golden Dawn, of studying books on Ancient Egypt and Atlantis (both common interests among the esoterically minded of that time) and also her love of the details in nature. The scene would be incomplete without the mention of the hollyhocks, and the wasps hovering over the jam pot. It also reveals her interest in the Baconian conspiracy. It is clear, therefore, that Mrs de Ward is a reflection of Nesbit herself, and such a mother is bound to produce a son who does not quite fit the expectations of society. When he is sent to school in Salisbury, Quentin soon runs away when he is bullied. Hitching a ride on a farm cart, he finds himself at Stonehenge at night fall on Midsummer Eve, and remembers his mother telling him about a girl who spent the night sleeping on the altar stone (most likely an allusion to Hardy's *Tess*). He picks a handful of 'the magic flower' St John's

Wort, and settles down to sleep on the 'smooth, solid, steady stone'. But it is when Quentin awakes that things start to get more clearly esoteric. He awakes on a ship, transported (he thinks) by accidental magic – a combination of the St John's Wort and spending Midsummer Eve asleep on the altar stone is responsible:

> He had read about magic, but he had not wholly believed in it, and yet, now, if this was not magic, what was it? You go to sleep on an old stone in a ruin. You wake on the same stone, quite new, on a ship. Magic, magic, if ever there was magic in this wonderful, mysterious world!

What makes Nesbit's kind of magic interesting to a Modern Pagan, is that this is no Enid Blyton *Magic Faraway Tree*-esque childhood magic. It has clear and powerful elements of much more ceremonial magic, with a scholarly interest and research behind it. The people that greet Quentin when he awakes are blue-robed priests of Poseidon from 'the great and immortal kingdom of Atlantis', a common interest for turn of the century esotericists, and, as is Nesbit's way, they speak a foreign language that the child is able to mysteriously understand. As he emerges from the purple tent that now surrounds the altar stone, the robed priests are saluting the sun. They invoke the 'sacred name of power', the 'sacred Tau', which name enables the speaker to command whoever they address, and decrees that the truth must be told. The chief priest informs Quentin that he is 'the chosen of the gods' and he tells Quentin that 'to the very last day of your life you have only to command and we obey'. However, it takes Quentin some time to realize that by becoming the chosen of the gods, this is the very last day of his life. He is now earmarked for sacrifice on the altar stone that brought him to this place, which is being transported to Salisbury Plain to complete the building of a new temple. His death will consecrate the new temple. Quentin tells the priest that the sun will 'strike through the arch on the altar stone at sunrise', and (in a reflection of our own Midsummer celebrations) 'the ruins are quite crowded sometimes, I believe'. Nesbit, whose own voice frequently steps out of the narrative mode to point out some useful fact or observation, then directs the reader to read Plato for a more comprehensive description of what Atlantis was like.

When the procession of celebrants (now dressed in white robes that symbolise ritual purity and with wreaths of pink London Pride flowers in their hair) arrives at Stonehenge, Quentin is surprised to see that the stones are 'overlaid with ornamental work, with vivid bright coloured paintings', in the same way that we now know the temples of Egypt or Greece were when they were newly built. Quentin is then directed to lie once more on the altar stone, as the rising sun starts to make its way across the temple towards the altar. The detail of the ceremony suggests that Nesbit is not merely writing fiction, but describing something she has experienced in a ceremonial setting, as a 'white robed priest with a deer-skin apron and a curious winged head-dress' steps forward holding a bronze knife, which he waves 'ten times in the shaft of sunlight that shot through the arch and onto the altar stone', saying, 'Thus do I bathe the sacred blade in the pure fountain of all light, all wisdom, all splendour. In the name of the ten kings, the ten virtues, the ten hopes, the ten fears I make my weapon clean.' It is worth noting that to the student of Western Hermetic systems such as that of the Golden Dawn, the significance of Nesbit's recurrent use of the number ten in this purification rite would be immediately obvious. In the system of Hermetic Kabbalah, the number ten represents the ten Sephiroth of the Kabbalistic Tree of Life. In simple terms these are emanations of the creative force of divine energy that pave the path to ultimate communion with the divine, and each degree within the Golden Dawn was numbered according to its place upon the path of the ten Sephiroth. The significance of ten is also mirrored in the tarot, since each suit continues from ace to ten. It is in these details of ritual that Nesbit's own interest in the esoteric starts to leak out into the narrative, ensuring the magic she describes is not just empty childhood imaginings, but the work of a skilled and well trained Hermeticist. *The Accidental Magic* draws to a conclusion as Quentin is offered in sacrifice to the gods. Just as he reaches the point of initiation into the mysteries and feels the point of the blade, he calls out for his mother, and speaking the 'word of compelling, the word of power', the accidental magic carries him once more home again.

The figure of the priest of the old gods who knows the secret word of power is a recurring in Nesbit's novels. In *The Story of the Amulet* (1905), the priestly figure appears once more, but this time he is a priest of Amen Ra. The book is filled with details of Ancient Egypt, right from the very beginning when Nesbit dedicates it to E.A. Wallis Budge, who translated *The Egyptian Book of the Dead* and was the keeper of Egyptian and Assyrian antiquities at the British Museum. Budge was also (to all accounts) sympathetic to members of the Hermetic Order of the Golden Dawn, and met with Nesbit a number of times when she was working on the book to assist her with her research. The details of the book are, again, authentic and based on actual research, and not merely fiction. For instance, the Amulet of the title is named Ur Hekau Setcheh, a real Egyptian name, and is inscribed with authentic hieroglyphics. The children of the story are helped by a 'poor learned gentleman', Jimmy, who is an Egyptologist and is probably based on the figure of Budge himself. Jimmy lives upstairs from them in the boarding house they are staying in while their parents are away, and helps them with historical and archaeological details when needed. He also accompanies them once in a while, although to his adult mind, he is convinced he has been dreaming when magical situations are revealed to him.

Again the motif of the children separated from their father

recurs, as he is away in Manchuria on war business (working for 'the tiresome paper he wrote for – the Daily Bellower, or something like that') and their mother is away in Madeira with the youngest sibling, the lamb, as she has been unwell. The children are therefore left in the care of their old cook in Bloomsbury, where they begin to explore the little streets around the British Museum. There they come across their old friend the Psammead, an elemental or sand fairy, who has been mistaken for a 'mangy monkey' and has found himself unfortunately for sale in an old curiosity shop. Once safely back in the custody of the children, he directs them to buy a broken Amulet, half of the Ur Hekau Setcheh, and they must go on various adventures while they seek to find its other half, and be granted their heart's desire for the family to be reunited. While the broken Amulet cannot grant them their heart's desire, it can act as a portal when the words of power are spoken, and thus it transports the children to various places that the Amulet has existed through time – Ancient Egypt, Babylon, the Phoenician city of Tyre, ancient Cornwall (the Tin Islands) and Atlantis, just before the flood occurs.

One of the most intriguing visits is to the future, when the children arrive in a utopian Bloomsbury, where H.G. Wells is venerated as a prophet (this book was clearly written before Wells tried to elope with Nesbit's adopted daughter). Future Bloomsbury is described lovingly in true Nature Mystic style, as the houses around the museum have been replaced with beautiful gardens:

> ...with trees and flowers and smooth green lawns, and not a single notice to tell you not to walk on the grass and not to destroy the trees and shrubs and not to pick the flowers. There were comfortable seats all about, and arbours covered with roses, and long, trellised walks, also rose-covered. Whispering, splashing fountains fell into full white marble basins, white statues gleamed among the leaves.

Even the pigeons are less mangy looking than London pigeons are now, as: '...the pigeons that swept about among the branches or pecked on the smooth, soft gravel were not black and tumbled like the Museum pigeons are now, but bright and clean and sleek as birds of new silver.' Also notable are Nesbit's aspirations for the people of the future, as both men and women care for the children: 'Everybody looked calm, no one seemed to be in a hurry, no one seemed to be anxious, or fretted, and though some did seem to be sad, not a single one looked worried.'

This view of the future owes much to Nesbit's political aspirations developed by the Fabian Society. Throughout the novel, there are also numerous references to the esoteric world. For example, the Queen of Babylon visits contemporary London and is mistaken for the Theosophist Annie Besant, who was a fellow Fabian and a close friend of Nesbit. And, as with *The Accidental Magic*, the details of the ceremonial magic invoked are quite astonishing. Somewhat more startling for children's fiction, towards the end of the novel, as the children have discovered how to re-unite the two halves of the Amulet, the 'learned gentleman' Jimmy undergoes a spiritual marriage with the ancient Egyptian priest Rekh-mara. The children cast a magic circle and invoke the words of power so that they can consult the Amulet (which is sentient once it is whole). Rekh-mara has become trapped in contemporary London and, unable to survive outside his own time and space, he can only live if a soul akin to his, and one of love, gives him refuge:

The children exchanged discouraged glances. But the eyes of Rekh-mara and the learned gentleman met, and were kind to each other, and promised each other many things, secret and sacred and very beautiful.

In a somewhat extraordinary piece of writing for the time, one of the children officiates the ceremony, and it represent a marriage of love as well as intellect and knowledge.

So Jane took the Amulet from Robert and held it up between the two men, and said, for the last time, the word of Power.

'Ur Hekau Setcheh.'

The perfect Amulet grew into a double arch; the two arches leaned to each other making a great A.

'A stands for Amen,' whispered Jane; 'what he was a priest of.'

'Hush!' breathed Anthea.

The great double arch glowed in and through the green light that had been there since the Name of Power had first been spoken – it glowed with a light more bright yet more soft than the other light – a glory and splendour and sweetness unspeakable. 'Come!' cried Rekh-mara, holding out his hands.

'Come!' cried the learned gentleman, and he also held out his hands.

Each moved forward under the glowing, glorious arch of the perfect Amulet. Then Rekh-mara quavered and shook, and as steel is drawn to a magnet he was drawn, under the arch of magic, nearer and nearer to the learned gentleman. And, as one drop of water mingles with another, when the window-glass is rain-wrinkled, as one quick-silver bead is drawn to another quick-silver bead, Rekh-mara, Divine Father of the Temple of Amen-Ra, was drawn into, slipped into, disappeared into, and was one with Jimmy, the good, the beloved, the learned gentleman.

Nesbit is clearly an author, Nature Mystic and esotericist who has long been overlooked. While her novels have remained in print since their first publication (which is quite a feat in itself) and scarcely a Christmas goes by without *The Railway Children* being performed in the West End or repeated on television, her remarkable place in the history of Modern Paganism is often overlooked. Whether or not this is due to the fact that she is principally remembered as a children's author, or because she was female, it would be difficult to surmise. Either way, she is worthy of much more attention from scholars of the esoteric.

Concluding Thoughts

The beauty of the myriad pagan paths that exist today lies in its diversity. Each person that embraces Modern Paganism as a way of life brings their own unique perspective to it, and there is no one body of text that has become canonised as 'the only way' to practice paganism. This allows Modern Paganism to change and grow with each generation of people who practice it, and makes it one of the more exciting faith paths, since it is what we make it. If one generation is not satisfied with the generation that came before, it is questioned, tweaked, re-written if necessary. And if one path within paganism doesn't fit, there are others. And if those paths do not fit, each individual can practice their own path. While to the outsider this can appear quite overwhelming and difficult to understand, it is also the element that keeps Modern Paganism developing and reaching more and more people as a possible life path.

For the purposes of this study, this growing and changing nature automatically makes this book quite narrow in its field of focus. I am quite clearly stating that the Nature Mystics in this series were not practicing Modern Paganism, since I have taken our starting off point (in line with the scholarship of Hutton) as being the repeal of the Witchcraft Act in 1951 and the publication of Gerald Gardner's *Witchcraft Today* in 1954. Doubtless there are those out there who are adamant that Modern Paganism developed before then, but their arguments are not convincing to me. The Nature Mystics explored here probably contributed to the cultural environment that allowed practitioners such as Gardner and Doreen Valiente to develop the belief systems that became Wicca, and also those other paths that emerged in Heathenism, Modern Druidry and the countless other nuances of Modern Paganism. To debate the origins of every path within Modern Paganism would take up far more space than is available here. This is a study of those writers who were curious about, inspired by, willing to explore and be transformed by the divine elements they saw in the natural world around them. While some may have been church-going, liturgy-responsive Nature Mystics, others eschewed the faith systems developed and spread through the organised religions, and instead preferred to sit amongst the violets, or underneath a tree they were particularly drawn to, to compose and write words that would in turn inspire future generations to connect and reconnect with those divine forces, both within (Human Nature Mystics) and without (Nature Mystics).

I also acknowledge with an open heart that this collection of writers is very narrow in its field of focus. While the turn of the century English literature is a field which particularly intrigues me, Modern Paganism has continued to be shaped and changed and influenced by writers before and after this period. There are countless others that could have been included in this line up, but the very nature of the 'Pagan Portals' series is to be an introduction, a short exploration. Perhaps by reading this, you might choose to explore your own favourite writers from a different perspective, one that acknowledges the formative power of the written word to shape and create our future, as well as to record our past.

Notes

1. Hutton, Ronald, 'Modern Pagan Festivals: A Study in the Nature of Tradition', Folklore, Vol. 119, No. 3 (December 2008) pp. 251-273, p 263.

2. Wunder, Jennifer, *Keats, Hermeticism, and the Secret Societies*, (Aldershot: Ashgate, 2008).

3. Curott, Phyllis, *Witch Crafting: A Spiritual Guide to Making Magic*, (London: Thorsons, 2002) p70.

4. Tianying Zang, 'D.H. Lawrence's Philosophy of Nature: An Eastern View' (Unpublished doctoral thesis, University of Northumbria at Newcastle, 2006).

5. So much so that I named a novel with one of its lines (*Somewhere She Is There*) and it featured in a piece of fiction about the process of initiation that was published in *Abraxas Journal I*, 'the Dark Flood'.

6. Kiek, Miranda, 'Elizabeth von Arnim: the Forgotten Feminist Who Is Flowering Again', *The Independent*, Tuesday 08 November 2011.

7. Graf, Susan Johnston *WB Yeats: Twentieth Century Magus* (York Beach: Samuel Weiser Inc., 2000) pxii.

8. Graf, Susan Johnston *WB Yeats: Twentieth Century Magus* (York Beach: Samuel Weiser Inc., 2000) P12.

Bibliography and Further Recommended Reading

Please note, where specific editions have been used I have given the publisher and publication date. Where books are out of copyright and freely available on e-book sites such as Project Guttenberg, I have just given the author name, title and the original publication date.

Butts, Mary *Ashe of Rings* (1925)

Butts, Mary *The Journals of Mary Butts* (Edited by Natalie Blondel) Yale University Press, 2000

Butts, Mary *With And Without Buttons* (Short Stories)

Butts, Mary, *The Crystal Cabinet: My Childhood At Salterns* (1937)

Coles, Gladys Mary, *Flower of Light* (Tiptree: Duckworth, 1978)

Curott, Phyllis, *Witch Crafting: A Spiritual Guide to Making Magic*, (London: Thorsons, 2002)

Davies, Owen *Cunning Folk: Popular Magic in English History* (London: Hambledon and London, 2003)

Gardner, Gerald, *Witchcraft Today* (1954)

Garrity, Jane, *Step Daughters of England: British Women Modernists and the National Imaginary* (Manchester: Manchester University Press, 2003)

George Mills Harper, *Yeats and the Occult* (London: Macmillan, 1975)

George Mills Harper, *Yeats's Golden Dawn* (London: Macmillan, 1974)

Gittings, Robert, *Selected Poems and Letters of Keats*, (London: Heinemann, 1986)

Graf, Susan Johnston *WB Yeats: Twentieth Century Magus* (York Beach: Samuel Weiser Inc., 2000) Greenwood, Susan, *The Nature of Magic: An Anthropology of Consciousness* (Oxford: Berg, 2005)

Hardy, Thomas *The Return of the Native* (narrated by Alan Rickman, which is an extra treat!)

Hardy, Thomas, *The Return of the Native* (1878)

Hardy, Thomas, *Tess of the D'Urbervilles: A Pure Woman Faithfully Presented* (1891)

Hutton, Ronald, 'Modern Pagan Festivals: A Study in the Nature of Tradition', *Folklore*, Vol. 119, No. 3 (December 2008)

Hutton, Ronald, *The Triumph of the Moon: A History of Modern Pagan Witchcraft* (Oxford: Oxford University Press, 1999)

Kiek, Miranda, 'Elizabeth von Arnim: the Forgotten Feminist Who Is Flowering Again', *The Independent*, Tuesday 08 November 2011

Lawrence, D.H. *Fantasia of the Unconscious* (1922)

Lawrence, D.H. *Poems: Selected and Introduced by Keith Sagar* (London: Penguin Books, 1987)

Lawrence, D.H. *The Fox* (Richmond, Surry: One World Classics, 2009)

Motion, Andrew, *Keats*, (London: Faber and Faber, 1997)

Nesbit, E, *The Story of the Amulet* (1906)

Nesbit, E, *The Accidental Magic; Or Don't Tell All You Know* (1912)

Radford, Andrew, *The Lost Girls: Demeter-Persephone And The Literary Imagination, 1850-1930* (Amsterdam / New York: Rodopi, 2007)

Susan Johnston Graf, *WB Yeats: Twentieth Century Magus* (Newburyport, MA: Red Wheel / Weiser, 2000)

Tianying Zang, 'D.H. Lawrence's Philosophy of Nature: An Eastern View' (Unpublished doctoral thesis, University of Northumbria at Newcastle, 2006).

Tolkien, J.R.R. *The Hobbit* (1936)

Tolkien, J.R.R. *The Lord of the Rings* (1954-1955)

Tomalin, Claire, *Thomas Hardy: The Time-Torn Man* (London: Penguin, 2007)

Townsend Warner, Sylvia, and Ackland, Valentine, *I'll Stand By You: The Letters of Sylvia Townsend Warner and Valentine Ackland*

(London: Pimlico, 1998)

Townsend Warner, Sylvia, *Lolly Willowes Or The Gentle Huntsman* (London: Virago, 2012)

Townsend Warner, Sylvia, *Mr Fortune's Maggot* (London: Virago, 1984)

Webb, Mary, *Gone to Earth* (London: Virago, 1979)

Webb, Mary, *Precious Bane*: with an introduction by Stanley Baldwin, and a new preface by Michelene Wandor (London: Virago, 1978)

Webb, Henry Bertram Law, *The Silences of the Moon (1911)*

Webb, Mary, *Seven for a Secret* (Teddington: The Echo Library, 2008)

Webb, Mary, *The Golden Arrow* (Teddington: The Echo Library, 2008)

Webb, Mary, *The House in Dormer Forest* (Teddington: The Echo Library, 2008)

Webb, Mary, *The Spring of Joy* (London: Jonathon Cape, 1946)

Wunder, Jennifer, *Keats, Hermeticism, and the Secret Societies,* (Aldershot: Ashgate, 2008)

Also by Rebecca Beattie

The Lychway
Somewhere She is There
The Softness of Water

MOON
BOOKS

Moon Books invites you to begin or deepen your encounter with
Paganism, in all its rich, creative, flourishing forms.